Rock and Roll Call

The History and Mystery
Behind Rock Names

ROCK
AND
ROLL CALL

The History and Mystery
Behind Rock Names

Dean Boland

Dowling Press

Rock and Roll Call:

The History and Mystery Behind Rock Names

Compiled by Dean Boland

For information address Dowling Press, Inc.,
1110 17th Avenue South, Suite 4, Nashville, TN 37212
First Edition
Cover Design by Art that Works

ISBN 0-9646452-9-7

*Featured on the cover: Janis Joplin, John Lennon, Tom Petty, Buddy Holly,
Mama Cass, Mick Jagger, Jerry Garcia, Courtney Love, Natalie Merchant and
Jimi Hendrix*

To my wife, Lisa,

a woman

who deserves

the very best...

Thankfully, she settled for me.

Acknowledgements

No list of persons to whom I owe thanks will be complete. But, I will not let that deter me from thanking all those that I can recall for their help with this book. First, thank God for overlooking the imperfections in me.

All of the following helped out in ways both large and small: My family, especially my mom and my brother Eric and his wife, Jenny—all those babysitting hours; Everyone at the Whitlatch, especially Mo, Shannon (not such a crazy idea anymore eh?), Sharon and sister Gail; Dowling Press, especially Maryglenn, for your enthusiasm and zest for this project from the first; Brian Cleary for your time, insight and advice about this whole being-an-author thing; Kristin Ban Tepper for help with some of the early research; the martial art of Soo Bahk Do Moo Duk Kwan without which I would never have obtained the discipline and drive to finish anything, much less a book; and Lisa and Abby for living with a type-A, obsessive-compulsive husband and father who loves you both dearly.

Preface

Rock and Roll Call: The History and Mystery Behind Rock Names. What you have here are stories—stories about how rock bands got their names, as simple as that.

The idea for this book started long before the actual research began. Since I was about eight or nine, I have wondered about the origin of rock band names. My earliest recollections were of my older brothers and the names of the groups they listened to. I remember standing outside my older brother's bedroom listening to loud music, while he and his cool friends had cool conversations about the cool music they listened to. I can vividly remember their conversations about Pink Floyd. It struck me as odd—how all these teenagers I idolized could be discussing, much less listening to, a group with the word "pink" in their name. It just didn't add up, so I set out to find the answers.

From that point on, I kept a mental inventory of these oddly-named groups, which added up in my head in a haphazard sort of way. The momentum for this book began in early 1996. This book is based on research from rock music encyclopedias, newspaper and magazine articles, artist interviews in various publications, hearsay, information from fans via e-mail and the world wide web, and from rock music folklore all integrated into one volume.

If you bought this book to use as a scholarly reference, sorry. Most of the stories are accurate. The ones that are not accurate are at least interesting or funny. If you think I got it wrong, let me know. I will be adding, supplementing and generally fixing the mistakes of this volume in all future editions—the ultimate work in progress.

To this day I still take a drive down Detroit Road here in my hometown of Lakewood, Ohio, to survey the names of groups playing at the local concert hall, The Phantasy. Long before Trent Reznor became famous as the founder of Nine Inch Nails, I wondered what Nine Inch Nails were as I read it on the Phantasy marquee. The same goes for Screaming Trees, Echo and the Bunnymen and others. One in particular that stands out in my mind was the Jehovah's Waitresses. I have often wished they had made it big, just so that "Jehovah's Waitresses" could have been as much a household name as The Beatles or The Rolling Stones. Their name typifies the modern naming of rock groups; it makes you think, wonder and laugh.

Whatever age, whatever background and whatever type of music you call your own, somewhere in this book your curiosity will satisfy your long unquenched thirst for the answer to that eternal rock-n-roll question—how *did* they get that name?

.38 SPECIAL

Early in the band's career, police often broke up their rehearsals assuming that the racket was caused by an out of control party. A .38 Special is a gun used by police.

? (QUESTION MARK) AND THE MYSTERIANS

The vocalist, allegedly never photographed without his sunglasses, had his name changed to "?" and the band's name "Mysterians" was taken from a Japanese science fiction B-movie of the same name.

10,000 MANIACS

The name 10,000 Maniacs actually came from *2,000 Maniacs,* a cult horror film misheard by one of the band members.

101ERS

This band's name was taken from the number of the torture room in George Orwell's novel *1984.*

10CC

According to the band, the average amount of semen in a male ejaculation measures approximately 9cc (cubic centiliters). They wanted to be just better than average, hence 10cc.

13TH FLOOR ELEVATORS

The name "The Elevators" was originally suggested by the group's lyricist Clementine Hall. The "13th" was added because most buildings at that time left off the 13th floor. Additionally, in some circles, "13" is slang for marijuana.

24-7 SPYZ

24-7 is slang for something a person does all the time—24 hours a day, seven days a week. The band was influenced by an eclectic sampling of other music and viewed themselves as "spies" of other musical styles.

311

311 is the police code for indecent exposure. Allegedly, the band was involved in an incident involving a midnight swim in a public pool without regulation swim garb. The band members, when asked, have differing interpretations of 311: Chad: Male Magic. Nick: Five friends making music. P-Nut: Friendship. SA: Ya mama. Tim: A number dictated to me by a higher intelligence.

A FLOCK OF SEAGULLS

This rock name was taken from the book *Jonathan Livingston Seagull,* by Richard Bach.

A-HA

Originally trying to find a Norwegian word that people would be able to say in English, band member Mags

Furuholem, suggested the name. The name originated from what Furuholem called a "terrible song," but turned out to be a "great name."

ABBA

This Swedish pop group got their name by combining the first letters of all the members' first names. Agnetha Faltskog, Benny Anderson, Bjorn Ulvaeus and Anni-Frid Lyngstad.

ABC

ABC wanted a name that would put them first in the phone directory and didn't tie them to any particular type of music. Also, they felt the name stood for nothing and everything.

AC/DC

The term AC/DC is neither satanic nor evil as some fans and critics have suggested. During an interview, guitarist Angus Young points out that AC/DC does not stand for "Against Christ/Demon Child" or anything similar. Apparently, Young's sister, Margaret, found the name AC/DC on the back of a vacuum cleaner.

ACE OF BASE

Computer wizards Jonas and Ulf came up with the name Ace of Base. They believed they were "the aces" and thought of a studio "as a base to work in, like a military base." Additionally, no one could pronounce or remember their original name, Technoir.

ADAM ANT

Adam Ant's break in show business came when Derek Jarman noticed him walking around with the word "Fuck" cut into his back with a razor blade, and cast him in his 1978 film *Jubilee*. Adam Ant chose his name to connect himself with The Beatles by using an insect, and Adam because "it was the first name."

AEROSMITH

Contrary to popular belief, they are not named after Sinclair Lewis's classic novel, *Arrowsmith*. Lead singer Steven Tyler stated in a *Rolling Stone* interview, "That was just some book that they made you read in high school." Tyler claims he chose the word because it "sounded cool."

AIR SUPPLY

Member Graham Russell, who is "spiritually in tune" believes that after weeks of trying to find the perfect name, "Air Supply" came to him in a dream. There are several different meanings: Air is a term in classical music meaning "melody"—At the time (late seventies) everyone else in Australia seemed to be doing heavy metal, so their music was "a breath of fresh air."—Both Graham Russell and

Russell Hitchcock are Geminis, which is an air sign, and they figured it would sound hip.

THE ALARM

To come up with their name, band members threw ideas into a hat. One member began telling the others about a song that he had written called "Alarm Alarm." The group soon after realized that there was already a Duran Duran and Talk Talk so they dropped the second Alarm.

ALICE COOPER

Born Vincent Furnier, when asked about the name change, he stated, "I have no idea. I really don't."

ALICE IN CHAINS

"We met pretty much by coincidence," Jerry Cantrell said. "I showed up at a party once, and Layne [Staley] invited me up to see his band rehearse. They were called Flea, and later they changed the name to Alice in Chains. We stole the name years later. It was basically through Layne that I met Mike and Sean." A second story states that while band members watched the television show *The Honeymooners*, Ralph Kramden, played by Jackie Gleason, said he'd like to see Alice in chains.

ALL ABOUT EVE

The title of a 1950 Bette Davis movie about an aging Broadway star became this band's name.

ALPHAVILLE
Band members took their name from the 1965 Jean Luc Godard directed science fiction film.

THE AMBOY DUKES
The name was stolen by founding member, Ted Nugent, from a then-defunct Detroit band. Starting over in Chicago, Nugent thought he would use the name since the original band wasn't even together. Amboy Dukes actually refers to a 1950s gang in New Jersey as well as a pulp novel of the same name.

AMBROSIA
The members of Ambrosia chose the name because it connotes their vision of their music: all shades, textures, colors and styles. Additionally, ambrosia is the food of the gods in Greek mythology.

AMEN CORNER
Named for the section of the Negro spiritual church where a group of women sat and hollered the "Amens." The Amen Corner is also the nickname for an exceptionally difficult hole on the golf course in Augusta, Georgia, which hosts the annual Masters Golf Tournament.

AMERICA
The band's name developed from many sources, including homesickness for the US. (They were children of overseas military personnel). When they noticed a jukebox with the "Americana" label, they deleted the final "a" and made it their permanent name.

THE AMERICAN BREED
This band was named after a breed of cattle developed by Art Jones on his ranch near Portales, New Mexico. This breed is composed of one half Brahma, one eighth bison, one quarter Charlois, one sixteenth Hereford, and one sixteenth Shorthorn.

THE ANIMALS
The band named themselves after a colorful member, "Animal," of a street gang they were involved with while in their early teens.

ANTHRAX
Anthrax is a fatal infection usually found in cows and sheep. Guitarist Scott Ian selected the name after hearing about the disease in high school.

APRIL WINE
According to the band's web page, the name was coined by member David Henman for "no apparent reason."

ARCADIA
Named after the central region of the Greek Peloponnese which was the home of the god Pan.

ART OF NOISE
The group's name was selected by Trevor Horn from an essay by Italian futurist Luigi Russolo published in 1913.

ASIA
Their name was suggested by the band's manager. They wanted the name to cause people to wonder what it meant and who the group was.

THE ASSOCIATION
Band member Terry Kirkman's wife accidentally happened upon the word "association" while trying to locate the definition of the word "aristocrat" which the band was thinking of using.

ASWAD
Aswad is the word for black in Amharic, an Ethiopian language.

ATLANTA RHYTHM SECTION
The band formed in 1970 in Doraville, Georgia. Band members came up with the name Atlanta Rhythm Section

Rock and Roll Call

because they spent most of their time in recording sessions in Atlanta playing rhythm for various musicians before they got together as a group.

AVERAGE WHITE BAND

The name "Average White Band" was a tongue-in-cheek comment on the group's all white, yet soulful sound. They kept their name even after a black drummer joined the band in 1975.

AZTEC CAMERA

According to the band's manager, Bob Johnson, Roddy Frame, who originated the band, selected the name for the psychedelic quality of the phrase.

B.B. KING

Born Riley B. King, he had his own radio show from 1949-1950 in which he was introduced as "The Beale Street Blues Boy." Later the name was shortened to "Blues Boy" and finally to B.B.

THE B-52S

B-52 is a reference to a bomber in the US military arsenal. B-52 is also the name of the hairstyle female band members Kate Pierson and Cindy Wilson wear.

BABES IN TOYLAND

The name is a reference to an operetta by Victor Herbert that was made into a film by Laurel and Hardy in 1934 and then by Disney in 1961.

BACHMAN TURNER OVERDRIVE

Originally, the band called itself Brave Belt, which referred to the belt an Indian brave wore to hang his scalps on during and after battle. Their record company suggested they use their own names like Crosby, Stills & Nash, and Seals & Crofts had done. They began calling themselves Bachman Turner, a combination of two group members' last names. To emphasize their heavy rock music sound, they chose to add the word "overdrive" after seeing a magazine by the same name in a gas station in Canada.

BAD COMPANY

This name came from the 1972 film of the same name starring Jeff Bridges.

BAD ENGLISH

The name was coined when band members Neal Schon and Jon Cain were playing pool and tried a shot with some spin or "English" on it. The shot, apparently unsuccessful, merited the comment, "That's bad English," which subsequently became the band's name.

BAD RELIGION

The name was selected by the then-teenage members to upset adults. The name was also a response to the popularity of televangelism.

BADFINGER

Allegedly, the band was named by the head of Apple Records after a blues tune called "Badfinger Boogie."

BANANARAMA

In an interview in the *San Diego Tribune*, a member told the following story: "The 'rama' part of their name was inspired by a Roxy Music tune; the banana part was just for laughs." A second story has the name being a hybrid of "The Banana Splits," a 1960's children's television show and "Pyjamarama," a Roxy Music song.

THE BAND

After working with Bob Dylan at Woodstock, everyone began to refer to the backup group as "The Band." The name stuck.

BANGLES

Originally, the band called themselves the Bangs and began playing on the LA club circuit. Unfortunatley, another group in New Jersey was already using The Bangs. The other group also had good lawyers, and the Bangs became the Bangles. A second story states that the group, originally called the Bangs, changed their name to the Bangles after the Electric Prune's song of the same name.

BARENAKED LADIES
Band member Ed Robertson explained on the television show *MuchMusic* that the name is "sexual, but it's not sexist. It's supposed to represent the feelings of innocence and discovery a little kid might experience on seeing his first barenaked lady."

BARRACUDAS
This group took their name from the Standell's song "Barracuda."

BAUHAUS
Literally translated, it means "architecture house" and refers to a German school for the study of architecture.

BAY CITY ROLLERS
The manager of the band stuck a pin into a United States map and it landed on Bay City, Michigan, incidentally, Madonna's hometown.

BB & Q BAND
BB&Q is an abbreviation of the Brooklyn, Bronx and Queens Band.

BEACH BOYS

Originally called the Pendletones, they discovered their new name while looking at the cover of one of their first records. The band anticipated the record would say The Pendletones. Only after the record was produced and the cover created did they realize that the record company had changed their name to The Beach Boys in an effort to package them with other surfing acts popular at the time.

BEASTIE BOYS

Beastie stands for Boys Entering Anarchistic States Towards Inner Excellence.

BEATLES

The boys thought that the name Buddy Holly and the Crickets was cool because the word "cricket" in England was a pun meaning both an insect and a game. The name "Beatles" was chosen to have the same effect; a pun meaning both an insect and having the musical term "beat" in it. Also, John Lennon used to tell the fictitious tale of how the Beatles' name came to him in a dream in which a man on a flaming pie said "You should be Beatles with an A."

THE BEAUTIFUL SOUTH

The phrase "The Beautiful South" is meant as a sarcastic reference to an economically depressed area in England—South London.

THE BEE GEES

Originally the Rattlesnakes, they were renamed the Bee Gees after their music began to get popular in Australia. A friend of the band, Bill Good, had introduced them to a local DJ named Bill Gates who started building their popularity. Once they became known, Good renamed them the Bee Gees after his and Gates's initials. A second story has the name coming from the phrase "The Brothers Gibb" a takeoff on "The Brothers Grimm."

BELLY

The band was dubbed Belly because it was lead singer Donelly's favorite word because it is "soft, warm and feminine."

BERLIN

John Crawford came up with the name to represent the original concept he had for the band. He wanted a European synth sound as some of his earlier influences were Kraftwerk, a German band, and Ultravox. In an interview, guitarist Ric Olsen cites the name's source as being derived from a "fascination with decadent pre-war Germany."

BETTER THAN EZRA

A reference to Ezra Pound in a quote from Hemingway's *A Movable Feast*—"I had heard complaining all my life. I found I could go on writing and that it was no worse than other noises, certainly better than Ezra learning to play the bassoon."

A second story: Ezra was a Jewish scribe and prophet of the 5th century BC, who with Nehemiah led the revival of Judaism in Palestine. In order for a band to be better than Ezra, they'd have to be really good.

A third story: Ezra refers to the bourbon called "Ezra Brooks." Therefore, listening to the band would be better than drinking this. Reportedly other brands of bourbon like Jack Daniels are sometimes used in phrases like "Better than Jack" to describe an action or event.

A fourth story: The term Ezra refers to a god of Greek mythology. This would suggest that BTE deserves godlike praise and worship.

A fifth story: The lead singer said during an MTV interview that Ezra was a positive state of mind, thus Better Than Ezra.

A sixth story: The name came from *National Lampoon* magazine. There was an article called "What To Call Your Band" and they chose to combine two of the names offered: Better Than Hendrix, and The Ezra Pounders (referring to the poet).

A seventh story: On KROQ's Love Line (a radio show in LA) the band mentioned that Ezra refers to some part of the body.

An eighth story: BTE was in a "Battle of the Bands" type contest. The first band was called "Ezra," so when

BTE won the contest, they took the name "Better Than Ezra."

BETTIE SERVEERT

This name came from a 1960's instruction manual by Dutch tennis player Bettie Stöve. Translated into English the name means "Bettie serves."

BIG AUDIO DYNAMITE

After deciding to use the acronym B.A.D. for the band, Mick Jones, formerly of the Clash, chose this expansion of the acronym from several other options.

BIG BLACK

Founding member Steve Albini said that he chose the name because it represented to him all that was scary and ominous in history. He felt that the name underscored that most historical images of fear are big and black.

BIG BROTHER AND THE HOLDING COMPANY

Big Brother is a reference to the tyrant in George Orwell's novel *1984*, published around the time of the group's founding and "holding" is slang for possessing drugs.

BIG COUNTRY

The name was selected because "it just implied a sense of vastness, open spaces—a sense of new discovery—a sense of ambition," according to Stuart Anderson.

BIG HEAD TODD AND THE MONSTERS

The band's name has nothing to do with Todd Mohr's hat size. Rather, the name is a tribute to the trio's blues heroes, like Eddie "Cleanhead" Vinson and "Fat Head" Newman. The band was playing a frat house one night and needed a name.

BIG STAR

The band took their name from the Big Star Food Market which was across the street from the recording studio where they recorded their first album.

BLACK CROWES

The name comes from a children's book, *Mr. Crowe's Garden,* that is a favorite of some of the band members. A second story tells that George Drakoulias spotted the band at a New York gig in 1988 playing under the name Mr. Crowe's Garden. He moved the band to LA after leaving A&M and changed the name to The Black Crowes.

BLACK FLAG

The name was selected because it connoted anarchy and implied the aggressiveness of Black Flag bug spray. The bug spray originally contained nicotine as its primary lethal ingredient. A drop of nicotine in liquid form is sufficient to kill an adult in minutes. The black flag is also the international symbol for anarchy.

BLACK OAK ARKANSAS
The group's members came from Black Oak, Arkansas.

BLACK SABBATH
The band's original name was Earth, which was in use by another group. Black Sabbath was chosen by drummer Terry Butler and inspired by a Denis Wheatley novel on the occult. A second story: While rehearsing in Birmingham, a cinema across the street was playing the movie *Black Sabbath*. They decided that if people were willing to stand in line to see a scary movie, then the band would write music to scare people. Subsequently, they wrote a song called "Black Sabbath." Later, Geezer came up with the idea to call the band by the same name.

BLACK UHURU
Uhuru is Swahili for "freedom."

BLIND FAITH
Eric Clapton chose the name in reference to the media hype of "supergroups" in vogue at that time.

BLIND MELON

This name came from bassist Brad Smith, whose Mississippi neighbors were unemployed hippies who called each other "blind melons."

BLONDIE

The name came from the cartoon strip about the escapades of Blondie, the dizzy blond, and Dagwood.

BLOOD, SWEAT & TEARS

The band was supposedly named after an incident in which keyboardist Al Kooper cut his finger during a show on a dark stage. When the lights came up at the conclusion of the show, Kooper noticed that his keyboard was covered with blood and he remarked that this would make a great album cover for a band called Blood, Sweat & Tears. Another possibility is that the name is taken from a 1940 speech by Winston Churchill.

BLOODSTONE

The lead singer named the group after a type of rock called a bloodstone.

BLOW MONKEYS

In his teens, singer Dr. Robert lived in Australia where he heard the expression used to refer to Aboriginal didgeridoo players.

BLUE OYSTER CULT

The name is an anagram of "Cully Stout Beer." It was chosen by one of the band members as they sat drinking with their manager one night and rearranging the letters in the beer's name.

BLUE RONDO A LA TURK

The band's name is actually a jazz piece, the most popular version of which is recorded by David "Take Five" Brubeck.

BLUES TRAVELER

On the music show *House of Blues*, the band's lead singer, John Popper said that the word "blues" came from the movie *The Blues Brothers* starring John Belushi and Dan Aykroyd. The word "Traveler" came from the character Gozar the Traveler in *Ghostbusters*.

GARY "US" BONDS

Frank J. Guida, Gary's original manager, convinced Gary Anderson to change his name to "US Bonds" thinking that radio stations would mistake it for a public service announcement and at the very least give their record a spin.

BONEY M

The name is taken from an Australian TV detective.

BOOKER T AND THE MGS

This name refers to band member Booker T. Jones and his backup group—the Memphis Group.

BOOMTOWN RATS

Boomtown Rats is the name of a gang in Woody Guthrie's autobiography, *Bound for Glory*.

BOSTON

Many people claim to have created the name, but no single story has an edge. However, founding member, Tom Scholz, does claim to have approved the name from many other suggestions.

BOW WOW WOW

Malcolm McLaren, the group's manager, named the band in honor of Nipper, the trademark dog of RCA.

DAVID BOWIE

Born David Jones, he changed Jones to Bowie after the "Bowie" knife and to avoid confusion with Davy Jones of the Monkees.

BREAD

This group's name was changed to Bread after the band got stuck in traffic behind a Wonderbread truck.

THE BREEDERS

Allegedly, "breeders" is a derogatory term for heterosexuals that was popular in the homosexual community during the time the group was looking for a name.

BRILLIANT

The band chose their name hoping that disc jockeys would announce, "That was Brilliant."

BROWNSVILLE STATION

The band's drummer, T.J. Cronley, suggested the name because the band played a lot of Southern rock. The southernmost city, Cronley reasoned, is Brownsville, Texas.

THE BUCKINGHAMS

The band formed in 1965 and went under contract to appear on a television show in Chicago. The producers wanted them to have a British-sounding name, so a security guard at the station suggested the Buckinghams.

BUCKS FIZZ

A bucks fizz is a cocktail of champagne and orange juice.

BUFFALO SPRINGFIELD

Band members saw the name on the side of a steamroller. Buffalo Springfield was the name of the steamroller's manufacturer.

THE BUGGLES

Formed by Trevor Horn in the 1970s in England, the group selected what they believed would be the most disgusting name possible.

BUSH

According to the group, the name was chosen because of the word's different English meanings. In particular, bush is a slang term for marijuana, as well as for female genitalia. Additionally, the group lives near a place called Shepherd's Bush and one of the group's members liked the 'shhh' at the end of the word.

THE BUTTHOLE SURFERS

For each successive gig, the band frequently changed their name to something as outrageous as they could. While preparing to play a song called "The Butthole Surfers" one night in a club, the group was mistakenly introduced as the Butthole Surfers and the name stuck.

BUZZCOCKS

This name came from the catch phrase of a character in the TV series "Rock Follies" who often said, "Give me a buzz, cock."

THE BYRDS

The name was chosen to fit in with the band naming trend of the time—B-words like the Beatles, Beach Boys, etc. seemed popular—so they chose the name The Byrds. They changed the spelling to distinguish the name.

CABARET VOLTAIRE

Taken from the Zurich cafe that was the headquarters for the Swiss dadaists leading up to W.W.I.

CAKE

Reportedly, cake is a reference to "caked with mud" rather than birthday cake.

CAMPER VAN BEETHOVEN

The name was offered by guitarist David McDaniel. No one knows why he chose it.

CAN

In Julian Cope's book, *Krautrock,* he mentions that the word "can" has several meanings. One member of the group defined "can" as an acronym for Communist Anarchy Nation.

CANDLEBOX

The band chose Candlebox after a line in a song by the group Midnight Oil, "boxed in like candles."

CANNED HEAT

The band took their name from a song by country singer Tommy Johnson.

THE CAPTAIN & TENNILLE

Daryl Dragon (AKA "The Captain") responded via e-mail with the following story:

"The origin of the name 'The Captain' came from my working with The Beach Boys between the years 1967 and 1972. Around the year 1969, I purchased a Captain's hat at a war surplus store, put it on, and kept it on during the Beach Boys' show. I told Mike Love of The Beach Boys that my stage name was 'Captain Keyboard' since I played piano and synths for them. He remembered the title and when I was given a solo on 'Help Me Rhonda,' he announced to the audience that Captain Keyboard was doing a solo. I jumped up and down wildly while doing the solo and the people liked that. I continued to wear the hat on stage with The Beach Boys.

The other reason I named myself The Captain when we (Captain and Tennille) got a record deal was because I did not want to use my real name, Daryl Dragon. During the 1950s and 1960s and even the 1970s, my father, Carmen Dragon, was well known in the music industry as a renowned symphony conductor, musical arranger and conductor. If a son or daughter of a famous entertainer or celebrity tries to get into show business, the entertainment industry tends to believe that the parent helped them get there and that the child's talent is probably minimal. Therefore, I chose not to use my real name."

CAPTAIN BEEFHEART

Band member Don Van Vliet was a classmate of Frank Zappa's at Antelope Valley High School. Zappa nicknamed him Captain Beefheart because he seemed to have a "beef in his heart" against everyone.

THE CARS

A friend suggested the name and lead singer Ric Ocasek liked it because it was easy to spell and had a "z" sound at the end without using the letter "z."

THE CAVEDOGS

The name came from a term used by one of the members' high school English teachers. The teacher used the term "cavedog" in reference to a less than attractive woman.

THE CHAMPS

The name was taken from Gene Autry's horse, Champ.

THE CHANTELS

This group met singing in their high school choir. They took their name from a cross-town competitor, St. Francis de Chantelle.

Rock and Roll Call

THE CHARLATANS UK

The name was chosen at random from the dictionary. The UK was added to differentiate them from a US band already using the name.

CHEAP TRICK

In a 1980 appearance on the television show "Kids Are People Too" guitarist Rick Nielson claimed that they were at a promoter's house for dinner fooling around with a Ouija board. Someone asked the board what they were going to have for dinner and the board spelled "Cheap Trick." In an interview on VH1, Robin Zander claimed that he originally wanted to call the group "The Horny Bulls."

CHUBBY CHECKER

Born Ernest Evans, he was renamed Chubby Checker by Kal Mann, owner of Parkway Records, as a play on the name Fats Domino. Another story tells that Dick Clark's wife suggested the name after seeing him perform on American Bandstand.

THE CHI-LITES

The band was originally called the Hi-Lites, but the name was already taken by another band who threatened to sue them. They added the "C" to distinguish themselves.

CHICAGO

Originally named the Chicago Transit Authority, the band shortened the name to Chicago at the threat of a lawsuit.

CHICKEN SHACK

This group was named after the blues song "Chicken Shack Blues."

CINDERELLA

This name originated from a soft-porn movie some of the band members caught on cable.

THE CIRCLE JERKS

The name was chosen from an entry in the *American Slang Dictionary* relating to a form of group masturbation.

CLANNAD

The word clannad is Irish for "family."

THE CLASH

The band chose the name after seeing the word "clash" in several headlines in papers throughout the world during the preceding year.

THE COASTERS

The band was named in honor of the members' West Coast origins.

COCTEAU TWINS

The band is named after Jean Cocteau, a French artist and writer.

COLLECTIVE SOUL

This band took their name from a novel by Ayn Rand entitled *The Fountainhead*.

COMMANDER CODY AND HIS LOST PLANET AIRMEN

The band's name is a combination of *Commando Cody, Sky Marshal of the Universe* (a weekly serial shown at movie theaters in the 1940s) and *The Lost Planet Airmen*, another serial which was a compilation of outtakes from *Commando Cody*.

COMMODORES

Band member William King chose the name from the dictionary.

COMMUNARDS

This name refers to a gesture of solidarity with radical insurgents of the Paris Commune in 1870.

CONCRETE BLONDE

The band claims that Michael Stipe of R.E.M. came up with the name. They don't think even he knows what it means.

ELVIS COSTELLO
Born Declan MacManus, he was urged to change his name by his manager. In a *Rolling Stone* interview, Costello admitted that "it was just a marketing scheme."

COUNTING CROWS
The band's name was taken from a movie called *Signs of Life* starring Mary-Louise Parker. Reportedly, one of the band members dated her for a short time. The name is also an old rhyme that suggests that "life is as pointless as counting crows."

COUNTRY JOE AND THE FISH
The band was originally named "Country Mao and the Fish" after a quote by Chinese Communist leader Mao Tse Tung, which a member recited as: "revolutionaries move through the people like the fish through the sea." One member thought the name was a bit dumb so it was changed to Country Joe after Joseph Stalin.

THE COWBOY JUNKIES
The band chose the name to reflect the blending of country and blues sounds and because "it was attention-getting."

CRACKER

The word "cracker" is defined depending on what country / time zone / astral plain you inhabit. Cracker can be defined as:

a) A low-income white inhabitant of the Southern United States: It is generally derogatory in nature.

b)A thin dry biscuit.

c) A UK TV series featuring a fat, alcoholic criminal psychologist with marital problems.

d) The name of Jimmy Corkhill's dog on *Brookside,* a popular UK soap opera.

e) A joke. Irish comedian Frank Carson often repeats the phrase "It's a cracker!" ad nauseam.

f) A British Christmas novelty explosive device, usually pulled at meal-times and containing a small plastic toy and/or a joke (e.g. Where do you weigh a whale? At the whale-weigh station).

g) Leather, usually sheep-skin, trousers which were popular in South Africa in the 1800s.

h) A computer hacker who concentrates on breaking into program code to enable extra features. (Coincidentally, said hackers are often confused when they receive the band's newsletter.)

It is generally accepted that Cracker, the band, takes their name from definition a) above.

THE CRAMPS

Founding member Ivy Rorschach explained in an interview that the name was chosen because it sounded like a street gang and further explained, "In France it's slang for hard-on."

CRANBERRIES

Lawler and the Hogan brothers formed the Cranberries in 1990. The band was originally called The Cranberry Saw Us, but Lawler insists there's no significant story behind the name. "It was just a name that suited us." After meeting Delores O'Riordan they changed the name and started recording demo tapes.

CREAM

The name was suggested by Eric Clapton. Cream consisted of the three most talented musicians of the 1960's blues and rock scene. They considered themselves the "cream of the crop."

CREEDENCE CLEARWATER REVIVAL

Creedence was the purposeful misspelling of the first name of a friend of the band's members. Clearwater came from an Olympia beer commercial. Revival denoted a personal revival of the band members themselves.

THE CREW CUTS

Cleveland disc jockey Bill Randle convinced the band to change their name after seeing their hairstyles.

CROWDED HOUSE

The name was inspired by the cramped accommodations where band members lived in 1985 while rehearsing for their debut album in Hollywood.

THE CRYSTALS

The group was named after songwriter Larry Bates's daughter, Crystal.

THE CULT

Ian Astbury was originally in a band called Southern Death Cult whose name was taken from a headline in a local newspaper. Southern Death Cult disbanded and Ian formed a band with Billy Duffy and named it The Death Cult to carry on the familiarity with the name. Some time later, they decided to drop the "Death" and simply became The Cult.

CULTURE CLUB

This name is the final form of the band's former names— the Caravan Club and the Can't Wait Club.

THE CURE

This band changed their name from Easy Cure to reflect a less "hippy-ish" sound and to coincide with other bands sporting "the" in front of their names like The Clash, The Cult, The Alarm, etc.

CURVED AIR

The name was borrowed from *A Rainbow in Curved Air*, the title of a 1969 album by Terry Riley.

THE CYLINDERS

This group originally contained four members and was called "The Four Cylinders" after the popular four-cylinder car engine. One member dropped out so they opted for an abbreviated version of the name.

D GENERATION

Singer Jesse Malin was quoted in *Rolling Stone* as choosing the name "because we felt music and society and everything's degenerated and we said we're going to be the D Generation. It's a few plays on the words 'Dad, I'm degenerate...sorry.'"

DAMN YANKEES

The name came from founding member Ted Nugent's response when asked by a friend what he and Tommy Shaw (of Styx) could possibly sound like together: "A bunch of damn Yankees."

THE DAMNED

The name was inspired by singer Dave Vanian, a former gravedigger, who often performed in the outfit of the Transylvanian legend, Dracula.

DARLING BUDS

This band's name was borrowed from Shakespeare, Sonnet XVII: "Shall I compare thee to a summer's day?/Thou art more lovely and more temperate/ Rough winds do shake the darling buds of May/And summer's lease hath all too short a date."

DAS EFX

This rap duo of Andre "Dray" Weston and Willie "Skoob" Hines took DAS is an acronym for Dray and Skoob. Skoob's nickname is actually "books" spelled backwards.

DEACON BLUE

Deacon Blue was named after the Steely Dan song of the same name.

DEAD CAN DANCE

Band member Brendan Perry reportedly selected the name, which was inspired by "the transformation from inanimacy to animacy." This was reflected in an illustration on the album's cover, which depicted a ritual mask from New Guinea.

THE DEAD KENNEDYS

This name was chosen by lead singer Jello Biafra because it "provoked the most reaction." Apparently, other groups had thought of using it, but didn't have the nerve.

DEAD MILKMEN

The name came from the name of a mythical band a member used in a fan newsletter parody he had created in high school.

DEAD OR ALIVE

Originally called "Nightmares in Wax," the band changed its name in a panic ten minutes before a radio session. They hit upon "Dead Or Alive" because they couldn't bear the artsy names other Liverpool bands had chosen and did not want to be associated with that movement.

DEEP BLUE SOMETHING

Originally performing as Leper Messiah (from a line in David Bowie's "Ziggy Stardust"), the band realized that the name didn't quite work. Drummer John Kirtland explained, "[Lead Singer] Todd [Pipes] had this instrumental and asked what we should call the song. I said, 'Deep

Blue Something' expecting him to fill in the last word. Instead, he said, 'That's pretty cool,' and it became the name of the band."

DEEP PURPLE

The name was chosen at the urgings of guitarist Ritchie Blackmore's grandmother from her favorite song "Deep Purple," a 1963 hit for April Stevens and Nino Tempo.

DEF LEPPARD

This band took their name from a poster of a fake band lead singer Joe Elliott drew in art class. The name: Deaf Leopard. He thought the name was too similar to other English punk bands of the day. They didn't want punk rockers, a.k.a. "spikeys," showing up at their gigs so they changed the spelling.

DE LA SOUL

"De la" means "of the" in French. The translation of the name, therefore, is "of the soul."

THE DEL FUEGOS

Guitarist Dan Zane named the group after Tierra del Fuego, the southernmost point in the world north of Antarctica.

THE DEL LORDS

The name was chosen to have a 50's rock band/street gang connotation. Several bands, including the Del Bombers and the Del Diamonds, were using the "Del" prefix at the time. The band's founder, Scott Kempner, says the final straw was seeing an episode of The Three Stooges which ended with a writing, producing and directing credit to a man named Del Lord.

DEL SHANNON

Born Charles Weeden Westover, his name was created by combining the last name of his friend Mark Shannon and Del from his boss's car, a Coupe de Ville.

JOHN DENVER

Born John Deutschendorf, he decided to adopt a name that would be easier to pronounce. Denver, whose father was in the Air Force, moved frequently during his childhood. He eventually made Denver his permanent home.

DEPECHE MODE

The name was taken from a French fashion magazine of the same name.

DEREK AND THE DOMINOES

The name was selected just before Eric Clapton went on stage at the Lyceum in London. A fellow musician suggested they call themselves Del and the Dominoes, because he often called Clapton Del. Clapton switched the Del to Derek minutes before going on stage.

DEVO

The name was an abbreviation of the term "de-evolution," the theory that mankind is de-evolving.

DEXYS MIDNIGHT RUNNERS

This is a reference to Dexedrine, an illegal drug which allegedly boosts energy.

THE DICTATORS

Reportedly, the name was taken from the name of a fictional band that member Andy Shernoff wrote articles about in his ill-fated fanzine, *The Teenage Wasteland Gazette*.

DIE KREUZEN

The four band members were living together with a girl who annoyed them with her mantra of starting a band and calling it Die Kreuzen after a phrase in a German bible. She never used the name, so they did.

THE DILS

This band took their name from the name of a band in a poem written by one of the members in high school. The Dils is actually a shortened version of a fictitious band called the Cosmic Dilrod Troubadors.

DINOSAUR, JR.

Originally the band was called the Dinosaurs, but another band, already using the name, threatened to sue them so they added the Jr. to avoid problems.

DION AND THE BELMONTS

The band, which was formed by Dion DiMucci, was named after Belmont Avenue in the Bronx neighborhood where the members grew up.

THE DOOBIE BROTHERS

Doobie is a slang term for a marijuana cigarette.

THE DOORS

The name came from the Aldous Huxley novel *The Doors of Perception*, a book about experimentation with the drug mescaline. The book's title came from a line in a poem by William Blake: "There are things that are known and things that are unknown, in between the doors."

DR. DRE

While growing up in a Compton, California, housing project Andre Young won his nickname playing basketball and idolizing Dr. J.

DR. FEELGOOD

The name was taken from the 1962 song "Doctor Feel-Good" by Willie "Piano Red" Perryman.

Rock and Roll Call

DR. HOOK

The name was given after lead singer Rod Sawyer had to wear an eyepatch because of an injury sustained in a car accident. The patch and his pirate-like appearance spawned the name.

DRAMARAMA

The name was suggested to the band by a girl in a bar. The term refers to theater actors who take their roles too seriously and begin to stay in character in their regular life.

THE DREAM SYNDICATE

This name was taken from a Tony Conrad record, "Outside the Dream Syndicate."

THE DRIFTERS

Members of the band selected the name because they had drifted from one group to another.

DURAN DURAN

This band's name came from the name of a mad scientist played by Milo O'Shea in the 1968 Roger Vadim science fiction fantasy film *Barbarella*. The character played opposite Jane Fonda.

DURUTTI COLUMN

Formed in Manchester, England, the band named itself after an anarchist brigade in the Spanish Civil War.

BOB DYLAN

He was born Robert Zimmerman, but changed his name to Dylan in 1962. Contrary to popular rumor, Dylan did not change his name in honor of the Welsh poet Dylan Thomas. In an interview in the *Chicago Daily News,* Dylan reported that he changed his name because of an uncle named Dillion. He changed the spelling only because "it looked better." Another story suggests he changed his name in homage to Matt Dillon of "Gunsmoke."

EAGLES

Don Henley credits Glenn Frey with coming up with the name. The purpose of choosing the name The Eagles was to appeal to a wide audience and to have a name that wouldn't go out of style. Also, the band was interested in Indian folklore, mythology and religion at the time and the eagle was a sacred symbol in the Native American world. Eagles were responsible for transporting spirits from this world to the next and that symbolism appealed to the band members.

EARTH, WIND & FIRE

Founding member Maurice White's interest in Egyptology and mysticism spawned the band's name. Earth, Wind &

Fire comes from the three elements in White's astrological chart.

EASTERHOUSE

The band named themselves after a Glasgow housing estate.

ECHO AND THE BUNNYMEN

Band members chose the name to ensure that they would never take themselves too seriously.

EINSTURRZENDE NEUBAUTEN

The name is German for "collapsing new buildings." They chose the sound to describe their vision of their music as sounding like the noise created during destruction.

ELECTRIC LIGHT ORCHESTRA

The group's name came from Denny Laine's Electric String Band. There were a lot of 'light orchestras' during the sixties, which gave a different sound from the usual four-piece bands.

EMF

This band's name stands for the name of the groupies of New Order, The Epson Mad Funkers.

THE ENGLISH BEAT

The name "The Beat" was selected after guitarist Dave Wakeling found the word "beat" in *Roget's Thesaurus* under the entry for harmony. It was changed to the English Beat four months later when they realized that an American band already had taken the name.

ERASURE

The band has said that their name came from the David Lynch movie *Eraserhead*. Another story tells that a demo tape was mistakenly marked "Erasure." A third story is that they wrote a list of potential names which was circulated amongst friends and acquaintances for them to cross off the ones they didn't like. "Erasure" was the only name that was left.

THE ESCAPE CLUB

The band was named after a popular club in England located on the Brighton seafront.

EURYTHMICS

This name is defined in the dictionary as "the chronographic art of interpreting musical composition by a rhythmical, free-style graceful movement of the body in response to the rhythm of the music."

Rock and Roll Call

EVERCLEAR

Their name comes from the appearance of alcohol. The band used the name because alcohol looks harmless like water but when you drink it it's definitely not water. That's how they thought of themselves—fairly mainstream, but when you hear their music it gives you that kick.

EVERYTHING BUT THE GIRL

The band borrowed their name from a second-hand furniture shop in the city of Hull, where members Ben and Tracey were students.

EXTREME

The name was selected to reflect the group's spectrum of musical influences from Prince to Led Zeppelin.

FAIRPORT CONVENTION

The name was taken from the early meeting place of the band at Simon Nicol's Muswell Hill home.

FAITH NO MORE

This name was the same as either a greyhound or a thoroughbred members bet on and won a lot of money. Another story says the band was originally called Faith No Man, which was selected by a later-ousted singer for the band. Once the unwelcome singer was gone, they changed the name to Faith No More as a joke on the guy who was out of the band.

THE FALL

This band took their name from the Albert Camus novel of the same name.

THE FEELIES

In a 1988 *Time* magazine article, guitarist Bill Million was quoted as saying that the band "may have got the name subliminally from an old child's game: put your hands inside a covered box and guess what's inside."

FIAT LUX

The Latin translation for this band's name is "let there be light."

FILTER

The name was first suggested because one the members "liked the name." Filter was chosen because the group felt that it symbolized the mind functioning as a filter between consciousness and reality. Another member had also written a paper in college on the 19th century philosopher, Emmanuel Kant, who had a theory that the mind was just a filter.

FINE YOUNG CANNIBALS

The band named themselves after a sleazy soap-opera movie, *All the Fine Young Cannibals* (made in 1960 by MGM), starring Robert Wagner and Natalie Wood.

FIREHOSE

This name was inspired by a documentary in which Bob Dylan holds up a sign that reads "fIREHOSE" while the line "Carry 'round a firehose" from his song "Subterranean Homesick Blues" plays.

THE FIXX

Originally Jungle Bunny and the Banana Boat Boys, the band realized the potential insult the name carried and changed it. Their original choice of "The Fix" was altered, adding the additional "x" to placate their record company.

FLEETWOOD MAC

This name is a combination of the surnames of drummer Mick Fleetwood and bassist John McVie.

FLESH FOR LULU

The name came from the Scottish singer Lulu. The band was vegetarian and they saw her entering a local McDonald's. One of them summarized the incident with the phrase, "Flesh for Lulu," which became the band's name.

FLIPPER

This group's name is in reference to the popular 1960's US television series of the same name starring a dolphin.

FOGHAT

The name was formed while playing a word game, similar to Scrabble, during which one of the band members spelled out foghat.

FOO FIGHTERS

The band's name is taken from a World War II government code for UFOs.

FOREIGNER

This name was chosen because members of the band were citizens of both England and the United States.

FOUR SEASONS

This Frankie Valli-fronted group took its name from a Newark, New Jersey, bowling alley and lounge where the group had performed.

THE FOUR TOPS

Originally the Four Aims, the name was changed to avoid confusion with the Ames Brothers and because they were "aiming for the top."

FRANKIE GOES TO HOLLYWOOD

This group's name was derived from the headline of an article reporting on the movie-making plans of the young Frank Sinatra. The headline was hung on the wall of the group's rehearsal studio in Liverpool.

FREE

The name was suggested by Alexis Korner, an influential figure in R & B music in England in the 1960s.

THE FUGEES

Originally, the Tranzlator Crew, The Fugees is short for Refugees. All the group members trace their roots to Haiti, and the name is short for "Haitian Refugees."

THE FUGS

This name is taken from the term for "fuck" used in Norman Mailer's *The Naked and the Dead*.

GANG OF FOUR

Gang of Four refers to the group of political leaders who tried to gain power in China after Mao Tse Tung's death in 1976. Chiang Chiang, Mao Tse Tung's widow, was among them.

GAP BAND

This name comes from the initials of the three main streets in the group's hometown of Tulsa, Oklahoma—Greenwood, Archer and Pine.

GARBAGE

A friend of the band's came by the studio where they were doing a remix for Nine Inch Nails and announced, "This shit sounds like garbage." They knew that using 'shit' in the band's name was not a very good idea, so they settled on Garbage.

GARY PUCKETT AND THE UNION GAP

This band, formed by Gary Puckett, was named after his hometown, Union Gap, Washington.

GAYE BIKERS ON ACID

The band was named after the Ray Lowrie cartoon.

GENE LOVES JEZEBEL

Gene was one of the band members' nicknames and another member was in a film school project called Jezebel. The name was selected because of its theatrical sound.

GENERATION X

This name was taken from the 1964 book of the same name by Chris Hamblett and Jane Davidson, which reported youth opinions about sex, politics, drugs and religion.

GENESIS

The band's first producer, Jonathan King, gave them the name. He also suggested they write the concept album "from Genesis to Revelation." The term had more to do with the band's inability to choose a name as the release date of their first single approached. Jonathan King also viewed the release of the record as the genesis of his producing career.

THE GERMS

Chosen because it was a reference to the germination or start of something, the band sought to start something new in music and wanted it reflected in their name.

GILBERT O'SULLIVAN

This name is an ingenious combination of the names of composers Gilbert and Sullivan.

THE GIN BLOSSOMS

An apparent reference to a pretty flower, but actually a term which refers to a condition caused by excessive drinking that results in red cheeks and noses from broken capillaries. Allegedly, the band took the name from a description of W.C. Fields in Kenneth Anger's book *Hollywood Babylon*.

GLADYS KNIGHT AND THE PIPS

Pip is reportedly the nickname of a cousin of one of the group's members.

GLASS TIGER

In response to an e-mail query, Wayne Parker of Glass Tiger responded: "We wanted a name that covered both sides of the band. 'Glass' for the softer side and 'Tiger' for the harder side. P.S.—I am the harder side."

GO WEST

This name was taken from "Go West young man," a quote normally attributed to Horace Greeley. The quote is actually taken from an 1851 article by John Soule.

THE GO-BETWEENS

The group's name was borrowed from the 1970 movie, *The Go-Between*, starring Alan Bates and Julie Christie.

THE GO-GOS

Guitarist Jane Wiedlin thought of this name early one morning at the rock and roll Denny's on Sunset.

THE GODFATHERS

The name was taken from the Francis Ford Coppola film *The Godfather*. The title was found by a member while perusing *Halliwell's Film Guide*.

GOLDEN EARRING

This name was taken from an early song of the same name by the group.

Rock and Roll Call

GRAND FUNK RAILROAD

The band named themselves after Canada's Grand Trunk Railroad.

GRATEFUL DEAD

Originally called The Warlocks, the band picked a new name when they found that The Warlocks was already taken. Jerry Garcia randomly pointed to a page in the dictionary and the phrase "Grateful Dead" was under his finger.

GRAVITY KILLS

Doug found the phrase "gravity kills" while reading a political article in an issue of *Rolling Stone*.

GREEN DAY

The term Green Day derives from the band members' high school days. Green Days was their code for days in which they would all sit around and smoke pot.

THE GUESS WHO

This was a temporary name the band used for their first record until a contest winner would select their permanent name. The record was a #1 hit, so they canceled the contest and kept the name.

GUNS-N-ROSES

Led by Axl Rose, whose name is an anagram of oral sex, the name was taken from two bands that various group members had previously played in—LA Guns and Hollywood Rose.

GWAR

There are several stories about how this name was selected. First, when the members of GWAR first broke free from the iceberg in which they were imprisoned, they let go with a horrific scream: "GWARRRRRRR!" This was later shortened to "GWAR" and became the group's name. A second story is that the name is an acronym for "God, what a racket." Thirdly, GWAR members claimed that they took the name from a comic book as an acronym for "Gay Women Against Rape."

HAMMER

Hammer was born Stanley Kirk Burrell and originally called MC Hammer. The name Hammer was taken from a childhood nickname, "The Little Hammer," he earned while working as a bat boy for the Oakland A's

HAPPY MONDAYS

Guitarist Mark Day named the band after the hit "Blue Monday" by New Order. The New Order song was inspired by the suicide of the lead singer of Joy Division, Ian Curtis.

Rock and Roll Call

HARPERS BIZZARE

This name is taken from the fashion magazine.

HATFIELD AND THE NORTH

This band found their name on a road sign leading out of London.

HAWKWIND

The group's bassist, Lemmy (born Ian Kilmister), claimed that another member had a big nose like the beak of a bird and a gas problem, hence, Hawkwind.

THE HEARTBREAKERS

The band took their name from "Heartbreak Hotel" by Elvis Presley. They heard the song on a car radio and chose it immediately.

HEAVEN 17

Heaven 17 was the name of a fictional rock group in the Anthony Burgess novel, *A Clockwork Orange*.

HELMET

A friend of one of the band members suggested the name because of their fascination with all things German.

JIMI HENDRIX

Born Johnny Allen Hendrix, his name was changed to James Marshall Hendrix by his father when he was four years old.

HERMAN'S HERMITS

Peter Noone misheard another band member remark that he looked like the character "Sherman" from "The Adventures of Rocky and Bullwinkle" and decided to call himself Herman. The band was named the Hermits by a bartender.

HOLE

Singer Courtney Love named the band after a line in the play *Medea* by Euripides: "There is a hole burning deep inside me." She chose the name to confuse people.

THE HOLLIES

In the forward to *Crosby, Stills & Nash: The Authorized Biography*, Graham Nash wrote that "we were Buddy Holly crazy. So that's how our name came about."

BUDDY HOLLY

Buddy Holly was born Charles Hardin *Holley*, but his parents decided that is was too long a name for such a little boy. They decided to call him "Buddy," a nickname popular for the youngest in the family. The spelling of the last name was misspelled on a recording contract in 1956 and he never changed it back.

BUDDY HOLLY & THE CRICKETS
The name "The Crickets" came from a time when the band members were rehearsing in Buddy Holly's garage and kept hearing a noise they liked. That noise later turned out to be a cricket, hence the name.

HOLY BARBARIANS
The name was taken from Lawrence Lipton's book of the same name about Beatniks in California.

HOODOO GURUS
Guitarist Brad Shepherd stated in an interview that he always wanted to use the name Gurus. The word Hoodoo, which is from the vodun religion of West Africa, rhymed.

THE HOOTERS
An engineer in the studio mistakenly referred to the band's Hohner harmonica as "that hooter thing" when suggesting they add that instrument to a track.

HOOTIE AND THE BLOWFISH
The name comes from the nicknames of two of lead singer Darius Rucker's friends in college. He walked into a college party and remarked "Hey there's Hootie and the

Blowfish" and thought that would make a cool name for a band. Hootie was so named because he had big eyes like an owl. The Blowfish's nickname came from the look of his big cheeks.

HOT TUNA
Originally called Hot Shit, the band's record label required them to alter the name to Tuna.

HOTHOUSE FLOWERS
The story is that Liam was flipping through some old vinyl and saw a record called "Hothouse Flowers."

HUEY LEWIS AND THE NEWS
They were going to be called "Huey Lewis and the American Express," but another band had "American Express," so they were forced to change the name just before the release of their first album.

HUM
The band's choice for a name was between "Grendel's Arm" and "Hum."

THE HUMAN LEAGUE
This band's name came from the science fiction board game Star Force. The Human League is one of the two rival empires in the year 2180.

HUMBLE PIE

Suggested by guitarist Steve Marriot, the name was chosen by the band to counteract their media-propelled image as a "supergroup."

HÜSKER DÜ

The name was taken from a popular 1950's board game. Hüsker Dü means "Do you remember?" in Swedish.

ICEHOUSE

Originally called Flowers, the band renamed itself after they discovered that the international rights to the name Flowers were already taken by an Irish band.

THE ICICLE WORKS

This group's name was taken from a science fiction story by Frederick Pohl, *The Day the Icicle Works Closed*.

BILLY IDOL

Born Willen Wolfe Broad, he changed his name around the time his original band, Generation X, was formed. Apparently, one of his school teachers had described him as "idle." However, after toying with the name, he decided that "idol" was more appropriate.

IGGY (POP) AND THE STOOGES

"Iggy" is from James Osterman's membership in the Iguanas. The Stooges came from "The Three Stooges."

INDIGO GIRLS

The duo came up with the name when Amy Ray was thumbing through the "I" section of a dictionary. "It's a deep blue, a root—real earthy," Ray said.

INFORMATION SOCIETY

The term "Information Society" was coined long before the band ever existed, and was used to describe a society that revolved around information.

INXS

INXS is a phonetic rendering of "in excess."

IRON BUTTERFLY

In *The Encyclopedia of Pop, Rock and Soul*, keyboard player Doug Ingle gives the story behind the name: "I wanted a name we could live up to...heavy, tight; together, not only musically, but as people. It also means being light, dynamic, versatile and original. At the time, insect names seemed to be the big thing, so we became Iron Butterfly."

IRON MAIDEN

An iron maiden, which is a body-size shell with spikes on the inside, was a torture implement used in the Middle Ages. The victim was placed inside as the shell was slowly closed into them.

THE JAM

Reportedly, Paul Weller's sister thought up the name at the breakfast table: "Well, we have the bread and the marmalade, let's have the Jam."

JANE'S ADDICTION

Perry Farrell, now with Porno for Pyros, was quoted in *Interview* magazine with this story: "When I lived in LA originally, I was living in a house with between eight and thirteen kids....One day, this girl Jane appeared. Anyway, she ended up living in the room next to mine and we became close. When you invite someone like her out, and you come to get her and she's dancing in front of the mirror with a wig on, and there's nobody there, you gotta name a band after her."

JAPAN

Guitarist David Sylvain stated in a 1982 *Tourist's Guide to Japan* that the name was chosen "to get away from that rubbishy idea that a band's name has to give an idea of its music; our music had nothing to do with our name."

JEFFERSON AIRPLANE

The name is actually a slang term for a device used to hold marijuana cigarettes.

JESUS & MARY CHAIN
The band took their name from the offer on the back of a breakfast cereal box: "Please send away for a Jesus and Mary Chain."

JESUS JONES
While vacationing in Spain, one of the group's members remarked after looking in the local phone book that there were as many Jesuses in the Spanish phone book as there were Joneses in the US phone book. Therefore, Jesus Jones became the name.

JETHRO TULL
Jethro Tull was an 18th century English agriculturist who invented a useful farming device.

JEWEL
Her full name is Jewel Kilcher.

JO JO GUNNE
The name was taken from a character in a Chuck Berry song.

JOAN JETT AND THE BLACKHEARTS
The band chose the name because it would be catchy when written on a bathroom wall.

ELTON JOHN

Originally named Reginald Dwight, Elton John got his name by combining the names of two friends, John Baldry and Elton Dean.

JOHNNY HATES JAZZ

This name came from the Frank Sinatra song of the same name.

JOSEF K

The name is lifted from the Franz Kafka book *The Trial*.

JOURNEY

The group, then unnamed, ran a naming contest on KSAN radio but didn't like any of the suggestions from the fans. However, John Villanueva, a friend of Walter Herbert, the band's manager, suggested Journey, which the band members liked. They then made up a fictitious contest winner named Toby Pratt to prevent the radio station's listeners from revolting.

JOY DIVISION

The name came from the term for the prostitute's wing of a Nazi prison camp found in the novel *House of Dolls*.

JUDAS PRIEST

The group took their name from the Bob Dylan song, "The Ballad of Frankie Lee and Judas Priest" on his *John Wesley Harding* album.

KAJAGOOGOO

The group was originally called The Headstands after a change from Art Nouveau. The name was then changed to Kajagoogoo because it was a silly name that sounded like something a baby would say.

KANSAS

The band was composed of native Kansans.

KING CRIMSON

The name was suggested by the band's songwriter, Peter Sinfield. Guitarist Robert Fripp is quoted in a booklet accompanying the *Essential King Crimson* box set, "The name King Crimson is a synonym for Beelzebub, which is an anglicized form of the Arabic phrase 'B'il Sabab.' This means literally 'the man with an aim' and is the recognizable quality of King Crimson."

KING MISSILE

Suggested by a friend of the band, King Missile is a Japanese comic book character.

THE KINGSMEN

In 1958 the parents of the band's saxophonist hired an attorney to obtain the rights to the name from a recently dissolved band.

KINKS

Formerly known as the Ravens, the band picked the name from the phrase "Kinky," a slang word in the 1960s in London, meaning "attractively pervy."

KISS

The name came to one of the band members while driving his '63 Plymouth Grand Fury on the Long Island Expressway. Their name is not an acronym for "Knights In the Service of Satan," as has been rumored for years.

KISSING THE PINK

The phrase is from the game of snooker.

KLAATU

The band borrowed its name from the alien character in the 1951 sci-fi classic, *The Day the Earth Stood Still.*

THE KLF

An acronym for Kopyright Liberation Front.

THE KNACK

Vocalist Doug Fieger explained in an interview, "I started looking through the dictionary, and when I got to knack in the K section, I stopped. It was short, it was to the point, it had a neat sound, it started and ended with a K, which I thought was nice."

KOOL & THE GANG

Originally The Jazziacs, they became known as Kool and the Flames. They later changed Flames to Gang to avoid confusion with James Brown's Famous Flames. "Kool" was bassist and group leader Robert Bell's nickname.

KRAFTWERK

In German, kraftwerk means "power station."

KURSAAL FLIERS

This band was named after a train that passed along the front of UK's South End advertising the Kursaal Pleasure Park.

L.T.D.

The band's name stands for Love, Togetherness and Devotion.

L7

Band members selected the name because when it is written it creates a square shape. The band hoped they could be called either L7 or "square."

LAMBRETTAS

The band took their name from a motor scooter popular in the 1950s and 1960s.

THE LEAVES

The group took its name from a conversation between two of the group's members: "What's happening?" asked one member. "The leaves are happening," the other answered.

LED ZEPPELIN

This came about from Jimmy Page's early desire to set up a band with Keith Moon and John Entwistle of The Who. (At the time the two of them were thinking of leaving The Who.) Sarcastically, Entwistle reportedly remarked, "We'll call it Lead Zeppelin, because it'll go down like a lead balloon." The "a" was later deleted so that the mispronouncing Americans wouldn't call the group Lead (as in "lead the way") Zeppelin.

THE LEMONHEADS

Band guru Ivan Kreilkamp named the band the Lemonheads, after the popular lemon-flavored candy of the same name. Kreilkamp reportedly had a Lemonheads wrapper tacked on his bedroom wall.

LET'S ACTIVE

The phrase was taken from an issue of *Atlantic* magazine about the Japanese use of English in Japan and the accompanying syntax problems with some translations.

LEVEL 42

This name was taken from the answer "42" in the book *The HitchHiker's Guide To The Galaxy* by Douglas Adams. This is the answer to "the ultimate question of life the universe and everything."

THE LIGHTNING SEEDS

Taken from a line in a Prince song "The thunder drowns out what the lightning sees." Ian Broudie, the band's only member, misheard the line as "lightning seeds."

LINDISFARNE

Lindisfarne is the name of an island, a.k.a. Holy Island, off the coast of Northumberland (UK). A famous abbey was discovered there in 635 AD.

LITTLE FEAT

A reference to Lowell George's feet. George was often teased about his small feet by Jimmy Carl Black, a drummer for Frank Zappa's The Mothers Of Invention.

LITTLE RIVER BAND
The name was taken from a road sign in Australia directing motorists toward a small resort town, Little River.

LIVING COLOUR
The name was inspired by the introduction to the Walt Disney television show: "The following program is brought to you in living color."

LOOP
The name came from a little-known Velvet Underground track that shipped with an issue of *Aspen* magazine.

LOS LOBOS
In Spanish, the names translates as "the wolves."

LOVE
Originally the Grass Roots, the band changed their name upon discovering that another band had assumed the same name.

LOVE AND ROCKETS
The name was taken from a comic book.

LOVEMONGERS
Band members Ann and Nancy Wilson, also of Heart, chose the name. Lovemongers came from their feeling about the

world at the time. It was Lovemonger as opposed to War-monger.

LOVERBOY
Band members chose the name to get a reaction from fans and to stand out.

LOVIN' SPOONFUL
The name came from a phrase in a Mississippi John Hurt blues number—"I love my baby by the lovin' spoonful."

LUSCIOUS JACKSON
The band was named after the basketball player Lucious Jackson, whose name a band member found misspelled in a sports record book.

LYNYRD SKYNYRD
Band members named themselves after Leonard Skinner, a gym teacher at the group's high school who regularly harassed members of the band about their long hair.

MACHINEHEAD
Rumor is that the band took their name from a classic Deep Purple album of the same name.

MADNESS
The group took their name from an old hit by Prince Buster, a favorite of the band.

THE MAMAS AND PAPAS

Michelle Phillips recalled the origin of the name in her 1986 autobiography *California Dreamin'*. The name arose from a response by Sonny Barger, a local San Francisco Hell's Angel, being interviewed on the Les Crane show, a forerunner of the attack radio talk shows. Barger referred to the women in the Hell's Angels as Mamas. As the group watched the show, Cass Elliot seized on the word and someone else came up with the Papas as the name for the men in the group.

MANHATTAN TRANSFER

The name came from the novel by John Dos Passos about New York in the 1920s.

MANNHEIM STEAMROLLER

The group named themselves after Europe's mid-18th century Mannheim School.

BARRY MANILOW

On June 17, 1946, Barry Alan Pincus was born to Edna Manilow and Harold Pincus. When Barry Pincus was two, his father abandoned his family, leaving him in the care of his mother and grandparents. As a result, Barry adopted his mother's maiden name.

Dean Boland

THE MARCELS

The name refers to the "marcelled" hairstyle worn by several of the group's members.

MARILLION

Originally Silmarillion, the band borrowed the name from the title of a J.R.R. Tolkien book.

MARILYN MANSON

The band members' stage names are all composite names consisting of a first name of a female, and the last name of a famous serial murderer. Marilyn Manson: Marilyn Monroe and Charles Manson; Twiggy Ramirez: 1960's model Twiggy and Richard Ramirez; Madonna-Wayne Gacy: Madonna the singer and John Wayne Gacy. Ginger Fish: Ginger Rogers and cannibalistic killer Albert Fish. Zim Zum (the guitarist) is the only one who breaks this pattern.

MARSHALL TUCKER BAND

The band named itself in honor of Marshall Tucker, who was the piano tuner who owned the group's rehearsal hall.

MARTHA AND THE VANDELLAS

Lead singer Martha Reeves named the group in honor of Detroit's *Van* Dyke Street, and *Della* Reese, her favorite singer.

MATCHBOX
This band's name came from a Carl Perkins song, "Matchbox," which was recorded by the Beatles.

MC 900FT JESUS
The name was taken from a quote by televangelist Oral Roberts, who claimed a 900 foot Jesus came to him in a vision.

MC5
The name is a shortened version of their original name, the Motor City Five.

THE MCCOYS
The group took their name from the Ventures' 1960 instrumental "The McCoy," the b-side of the hit, "Walk Don't Run."

MEAT LOAF
Marvin Lee Aday was nicknamed Meat Loaf after stepping on the foot of his high school football coach.

MEAT PUPPETS
The name came from a cartoon by B. Klibin called "Bob & Jane See The All Meat Puppets." A second story tells that the band selected their name from a song they wrote which, according to band members, is about "what mindless fools

humans are." "Meat Puppet" is also television news slang for an anchorman or anchorwoman.

MEGADETH

The band was formed by Dave Mustaine after he was ousted from Metallica in 1983. According to Mustaine, "The band's name means the act of dying....to be more specific, one million deaths, or the hypothetical body count of a nuclear fallout."

THE MEKONS

The band took their name from an alien who terrorizes Earth in the 1950's English comic strip, "Dan Dare."

JOHN MELLENCAMP

Tony DeFries of MainMan Management landed a deal for John Mellencamp with MCA Records. When the album *Chensut Street Incident* was released, Mellencamp discovered that his name had been changed to John Cougar, courtesy of DeFries. In 1983, he added "Mellencamp" back to his name, but in 1991, dropped "Cougar" altogether.

MEN AT WORK

Men at Work got their name when they happened upon a "Men at Work" road sign.

MEN WITHOUT HATS

One story tells that the name came during a drunken night in a Montreal bar while members celebrated the recording of their first album. Another story is that the band wished to be uncategorized, and chose the name accordingly (i.e., "without hats," as opposed to "wearing many hats").

METALLICA

One of the group's founders, Lars Ulrich, had a friend who was looking for a name for a heavy metal fan magazine he was creating. When the friend suggested "Metallica," Lars liked it so much, he told his friend he didn't like it so that he could use it for his band's name.

MFSB

The band's name is an acronym for Mother, Father, Sister, Brother.

MIAMI SOUND MACHINE

In 1975, at the urgings of her mother, Gloria Estefan sang some songs with a band, The Miami Latin Boys, at a wedding. The band leader, Emilio Estefan (her future husband) was so impressed by her smooth alto voice that he persuaded her to join his band. She reluctantly agreed, but the band was no longer all male, so they were rechristened The Miami Sound Machine.

MI-SEX

This New Zealand band took their name from a song by Ultra Vox.

MIDNIGHT OIL

The band borrowed their name from the phrase "burning the midnight oil."

MIGHTY MIGHTY BOSSTONES

Originally the band called themselves The Bosstones in reference to their hometown, Boston. They later discovered that a band from the 1950s had used the same name, so they added "Mighty Mighty" to differentiate themselves.

MILLI VANILLI

The name was patterned after Scritti Politti, whom the band liked.

MINISTRY

Singer Al Jourgensen chose the name from a TV movie called *Ministry of Fear*.

MINUTEMEN

The name was chosen to underscore the band's rapid-fire songs which were usually played in their entirety in under a minute.

THE MIRACLES
Originally the Matadors, Berry Gordy insisted they change their name. The group's members placed suggestions in a hat and Smokey Robinson's offering was chosen by chance.

MITCH RYDER AND THE DETROIT WHEELS
Born William Levise, Jr., Mitch Ryder chose his name out of the phone book and picked Detroit Wheels to make them sound up to date.

MOBY GRAPE
The band's name is the punchline of the joke "What's purple and swims in the ocean?"

THE MODERN LOVERS
Jonathan Richman, who formed the band, chose the name to describe the type of songs the band would perform— love songs with a modern twist.

MOLLY HATCHET
The band was named after Hatchet Molly, an infamous lady of the evening who was known to castrate her clients.

MONKEES
The four were hired to star in a TV sitcom using their own names, but portraying a fictional rock band. The band was named by employees of the network.

MOODY BLUES
The name came from a Slim Harpo song.

MOTHER LOVE BONE
The band needed a new name. Bruce brought in Daddy Long Legs, and Stone came up with the Dum Dum Boys. But, it was Andy who eventually came up with the name Mother Love Bone. He spent a week trying to convince the rest of the group, repeating it at every practice. They finally gave in to him.

MOTHERS OF INVENTION
The group was originally called simply *The Mothers*. Their record company was concerned that the name might be some Oedipal reference so they added the phrase "of invention," taken from the old proverb "necessity is the mother of invention."

MÖTLEY CRÜE
The group got its name when someone passing them on the street commented, "Boy, that's a motley crew."

MOTORHEAD
The name is taken from the b-side of a 1974 Hawkwind single "Kings of Speed" and is also a slang term for an amateur mechanic.

Rock and Roll Call

MOTT THE HOOPLE

The band took their name from a Willard Manus novel.

MR. BIG

The group took their name from a song by the group Free.

MR. BUNGLE

Mr. Bungle was formed in Eureka, California, in 1985. The first incarnation of the band featured bassist Trevor Dunn, vocalist Michael Patton, guitarist Trey Spruance, drummer Jed Watts, and trumpet player Scott Fritz. Their name was taken from a short film on an episode of the Pee Wee Herman show, *Pee Wee's Playhouse*. The film featured an ill-mannered, unclean Mr. Bungle as a model of how children should not act.

MR. MISTER

In an interview in the *Chicago Tribune*, a group member was quoted as saying "I wish I had a good story for you about why we called the band Mr. Mister, but I don't. We knew from the beginning that we wanted to name it Mr. something. We thought that was good, but we couldn't come up with a second word. Finally, somebody yelled out, 'Why not Mr. Mister?' and we all laughed and said that's good enough."

MUD

They wanted a name that would stick.

MUNGO JERRY
The group took the name from a cat in T.S. Eliot's *Old Possum's Book of Practical Cats*.

MY BLOODY VALENTINE
The name was taken from a Canadian b-movie horror film.

NADA SURF
Nada Surf was a phrase used by writer Thomas Pynchon in a radio talk show in 1971, while still in college. He was trying to explain how Tibetan Monks should gain strength through "inner emptiness."

NAKED EYES
The band's name was taken from the phrase "to the naked eye."

NAKED LUNCH
The band named themselves after the William S. Burroughs novel, *Naked Lunch*.

NAZARETH
The name was inspired by the first line the song "The Weight" by The Band: "I pulled into Nazareth."

THE NAZZ
The name came from the b-side of a Yardbirds single called "The Nazz Are Blue."

NED'S ATOMIC DUSTBIN

The band found the name while looking through a book of scripts from "The Goon Show," a BBC comedy series featuring Spike Milligan and Peter Sellers.

NERF HERDER

The band borrowed their name from an insult used in the movie *The Empire Strikes Back*.

NEW ORDER

This name signified a fresh start for Joy Division after their lead singer, Ian Curtis, died.

NEW RIDERS OF THE PURPLE SAGE

This band's name is taken from a 1912 novel by fiction writer Zane Gray, *Riders of The Purple Sage*.

THE NEW YORK DOLLS

The band named themselves after New York, the city of their formation, and the book, *The Valley of the Dolls,* which is written by Jacqueline Susann.

NINE BELOW ZERO

The name came from a Sonny Boy Williamson blues track.

NINE INCH NAILS

Founded by Clevelander, Trent Reznor, the band's name comes from the nails used in the crucifixion of Christ.

NIRVANA

In a press release from DGC records, the late singer/songwriter Kurt Cobain offered the story behind the name: "It's saying, doing and playing what you want. In Webster's terms, nirvana means freedom from pain, suffering and the external world and that's pretty close to a definition of punk rock."

NO DOUBT

No Doubt's former co-vocalist John Spence (who committed suicide in 1987) coined the band's name. One of Spence's catch phrases was "no doubt."

NRBQ

The band's name is the initials for New Rhythm and Blues Quintet.

NUEROTIC OUTSIDERS

The purposefully misspelled name is adopted from an article about the *New Musical Express* alleging that the music magazine created a generation of "neurotic boy outsiders." The band deleted the "boy" and added a misspelling.

THE O'JAYS

Formed at McKinley High School in Canton, Ohio, as the Triumphs, they changed their name as a tribute to Eddie O'Jay, a Cleveland disc jockey.

Rock and Roll Call

OASIS

Liam saw a poster advertising a club called the "Swindon Oasis" and he thought Oasis would be a good name for a band. Other well-reported stories: 1. The first public place the Beatles ever played. 2. A leisure center in Manchester, England, the band's hometown. 3. The name of the cab service near a member's house.

THE OFFSPRING

The band considered themselves to be the second generation of punk rock, hence "offspring."

OINGO BOINGO

Originally a stage act called the Mystic Knights of the Oingo Boingo, they gradually added music and evolved into the band.

ORCHESTRAL MANOEUVRES IN THE DARK

The name was taken from the title of a song, written on band member Andy McCluskey's bedroom wall, which the band never recorded.

THE ORIOLES

Formed in Baltimore, the group named themselves after the city's baseball team.

OZZY OSBOURNE

Ozzy Osbourne was born John Michael Osbourne on December 3, 1948, in Birmingham, England.

THE OUTFIELD

Originally, the band called themselves The Baseball Boys, after the painted baseball-player themed gang in the movie *The Warriors*. They eventually signed with a manager who recommended a name change.

P.M. DAWN

The band derived their name from the saying that it is darkest just before dawn.

PANTERA

In Spanish, pantera translates to panther. The name is possibly a veiled reference to the members' hometown of Pantego, Texas.

PARLIAMENT/FUNKADELIC

Parliament comes from the brand of cigarette of the same name. George Clinton then coined the phrase 'funkadelic' by combining the words funk and psychedelic.

PAUL KELLY AND THE COLOURED GIRLS

This Australian group took their name from a line in Lou Reed's "Walk on the Wild Side."

PAUL REVERE AND THE RAIDERS

The real name of one of the band's members is Paul Revere Dick. The band chose the Raiders because it sounded like pirates.

PEARL JAM

The band's original name was Mookie Blaylock (after the NBA player). Eddie Vedder later suggested the name "Pearl Jam" in honor of his famous Aunt Pearl's home-made jam, allegedly a natural aphrodisiac containing peyote. "Pearl Jam" is also slang for semen.

PERE UBU

The name was taken from a character in Alfred Jarry's 1896 play, *Ubu Roi*.

PET SHOP BOYS

This band's name is rumored to be slang for a sexual act involving gerbils, which the band members decline to discuss. The band denies knowing this slang reference. They claim the name came from one of the band member's desires to work in a pet shop.

PINK FLOYD

Originally the Pink Floyd Sound, the band was named in honor of two Georgia bluesmen, Pink Anderson and Floyd Council.

THE PIXIES

Guitarist Joey Santiago chose the name at random from a dictionary.

POCO

Originally the band was named Pogo after the satirical cartoon strip by Walt Kelly. However, Kelly refused to allow the use of the name, so Poco was chosen because of its similarity to the original name and because in musical nomenclature, it means "a little."

POI DOG PONDERING

The band was formed in Hawaii, where "Poi Dog" is slang for mutt.

THE POLICE

Drummer and co-founder Stewart Copeland, whose father helped found the CIA, settled on the name before the band was formed. He hoped that cities around the world would give them free publicity, cop car escorts, station visits, etc. to assist with their gigs.

POP WILL EAT ITSELF

Allegedly, the band pulled their name from a line in an article about the future of music, written by David Quantick for a British magazine.

THE POGUES

An abbreviation of the phrase "pogue mahone" which is Irish for "kiss my arse."

PORNO FOR PYROS

Perry Farrell (a word play pronounced 'peripheral') claims that the band's name was coined when he found a fireworks advertisement while leafing through a magazine selling S&M videos.

PORTISHEAD

The band was named after founder Geoff Barrow's hometown.

PREFAB SPROUT

One story states that group leader Paddy MacAloon simply chose two words that had nothing to do with one another. He hoped people would then ask about the name. Another story has MacAloon mishearing the words "pepper sprout" in a Nancy Sinatra song.

THE PRESIDENTS OF THE UNITED STATES OF AMERICA

This band got their name at a party. During a performance, band members yelled out potential band names and chose the one that got the best crowd response.

PRETENDERS

The group took their name from the song "The Great Pretender," a 1956 hit by the Platters.

THE PRETTY THINGS

Named after the song "Pretty Thing" by Bo Diddley.

PRIMAL SCREAM

The band named themselves after a type of psychological therapy known as primal scream therapy.

PRIMITIVE RADIO GODS

Founder Chris O'Connor sent unsolicited copies of his self-produced CD, *Rocket,* which he attributed to a fictional band named Primitive Radio Gods after a song on the I-Rails' third album. The CD was sent to college radio, the music press and whatever industry executives he could find addresses for. Eventually, a record label called him in and signed him up.

PROCOL HARUM

Procol Harum, which in Latin means "beyond these things," was also the name of a friend's cat.

PRONG

Chosen because it was industrial-sounding, the name was taken from three-pronged plug.

THE PSYCHEDELIC FURS

The band settled on this name after pondering what nouns would go well with the word 'psychedelic.' The use of psychedelic was an attempt by the band to differentiate themselves from other popular bands of the time.

PUBLIC IMAGE, LTD.

Johnny Rotten started this group after the Sex Pistols broke up. He chose the name so that the group would be perceived as a company rather than a rock band.

PYLON

The band's name is taken from a novel by William Faulkner.

QUANTUM JUMP

This is a term used in physics.

QUARTERFLASH

The term comes from an Australian expression, "a quarter flash and three parts foolish."

QUEEN

The name "Queen" was lead singer Freddie Mercury's idea and was chosen because it was short, memorable and had the connotations of royalty, drama and dynamism.

QUEENSRYCHE

Originally, the band was called The Mob. Their self-financed demo included four songs: "Queen of the Reich," "Nightrider," "Blinded," and "The Lady Wore Black." The band's new name was taken from their song "Queen of the Reich."

QUICKSILVER MESSENGER SERVICE

The name was chosen because of the common astrological signs of the band members—Virgo and Gemini. In astrology, the ruling planet for Virgo and Gemini is Mercury. The element mercury is also known as quicksilver.

QUIET RIOT

The name Quiet Riot was suggested to singer Kevin DuBrow by a friend. DuBrow initially misheard his friend and asked why anyone would call a band "quite right." Once his friend pronounced the phrase with an English accent, DuBrow got it and used it as the band's name.

R.E.M.

The name was chosen from a list written by the band members on a chalkboard during a brainstorming session.

RADIOHEAD

The name Radiohead came about when one of the members was trying to listen to a football game while the band was practicing. A second story states the name was taken from the Talking Heads' song, "Radio Head," which was released in 1986.

RAGE AGAINST THE MACHINE

According to the band, their name refers to a people's movement of trying to push back the corporations, the governments, and empowered moralists from controlling our lives.

RAINBOW

Originally, the band was called "Ritchie Blackmore's Rainbow." The Rainbow portion of the name was borrowed from the Rainbow Bar & Grill, a popular spot in Los Angeles. Band members later decided they disliked having Blackmore's name in the band and changed their name to Rainbow.

RAMONES

In the early days of the Beatles, Paul McCartney briefly used the alias Paul Ramone, which band members borrowed for their name.

RATT

Originally called Mickey Rat from a character in a comic book, the band had to shorten their name to Ratt when the cartoon strip objected to the use of the name.

THE RAVENS

This band was named because everyone was "ravin'" about their sound.

RED HOT CHILI PEPPERS

Originally called Tony Flow and the Miraculously Majestic Masters of Mayhem, the band decided the name didn't do it for them and brainstormed until member Flea came up with this new one.

REDBONE

Redbone is a derogatory term used in Louisiana's Cajun country to refer to a bi-racial person.

REDD KROSS

This band's name is taken from the infamous masturbation scene in *The Exorcist* involving a crucifix.

REO SPEEDWAGON

The band was named after an old-fashioned high-speed fire engine.

THE REPLACEMENTS

This name was chosen after the group was thrown out of a local club. The club owner vowed to never let the group play in the town again, so they changed their name to the

Replacements to replace themselves and avoid detection by the miffed club owner.

RICH KIDS
The name is taken from a Jean Cocteau book.

RICHARD HELL AND THE VOIDOIDS
Richard Hell founded the group and added the Voidoids after creating the term during a contest with a friend at a local deli. The contest required both participants to create new words by placing various prefixes onto the suffix "oid."

RIGHTEOUS BROTHERS
Reportedly, they were named after an audience member shouted, "Hey that's really righteous, brothers," in response to their soulful singing.

ROLLING STONES
This group took their name from a song, "Rollin' Stone," by one of their idols, Muddy Waters.

THE RONETTES
The name was selected after Veronica Bennett's mother pointed out that the Bobbettes and the Marvelettes recently had hit songs. With a lot of "ettes" going around, they decided to join the trend.

ROXETTE

The band took their name from a 1970's Dr. Feelgood song titled "Roxette."

ROXY MUSIC

"It was intended to convey a slightly old-style glamour, with a pun on rock," stated lead singer Bryan Ferry. Another story is that "Roxy" came from the name of a hometown theater and the term "music" was added because another US band was already using "Roxy."

THE ROYAL TEENS

The group was named accordingly, because all the members were teenagers when the group was formed.

THE RUNAWAYS

The name was chosen by Joan Jett, who later left to form the Blackhearts. She claims there is no story behind the name.

RUSH

During the early 70s, some headshops in Toronto sold a product called "rush." The substance came in a small bottle and when sniffed, produced a head rush.

RUSTED ROOT

The band claims their name came from brainstorming. A second story states that one of the band members worked as a janitor at a factory that made nails and screws, and had to sweep up ones that had already rusted. Another future band member began to work there and they often played songs in a stairwell at the factory. When they considered names for the band, they went to the "roots" of the band. This combination spawned the name.

SAD CAFE

The band took their name from the title of the Carson McCullers book, *The Ballad of the Sad Cafe.*

SALT-N-PEPA

In a line from a song called "The Showstopper," the girls refer to themselves as "the Salt and Pepa MCs." When their next record, "I'll Take Your Man" was released in 1986, they had shortened the name.

SCORPIONS

When they were formed, there were already several other bands named after animals (The Beatles, The Monkees, etc.) and they decided to do something similar.

SCREAMING TREES

The name was lifted from one of the band's guitar effects pedals, the Screaming Tree treble booster.

SCRITTI POLITTI

Latin for political writings, the name later served as inspiration for Milli Vanilli.

SEARCHERS

The band was named after a 1956 John Wayne movie.

THE SELECTOR

This name was actually the title of the first song by the group The Specials that record companies refused to buy.

SEMISONIC

According to the biography on the band's home page, the name came from a quote: "I've had enough of this semisonic bullshit." They picked it as their new name since a funk band from the 1970s was threatening to sue them over their use of the name they had been using—Pleasure.

SEPULTURA

The word is Portuguese for grave.

SEVEN MARY THREE

They came up with the name watching the 1970's US cop show "C.H.I.P.S." on TV. The phrase "seven mary three" was a character's call sign.

SEX PISTOLS

The name was suggested by one of the founders of the group, Malcolm McLaren, as a distortion of the botanical term "pistils," which refers to a flower's male sexual organs.

SHAKESPEARE'S SISTER

The name was taken from a b-side track by The Smiths.

SHANGRI-LAS

"Shangri La" is another name for "paradise" in the James Hilton novel, *Lost Horizon.*

THE SHIRELLES

The name is a play on lead singer Shirley Alston's name.

SHONEN KNIFE

Shonen means "boy" in Japanese. No significance has been attributed to the combination of the word with "knife".

SHOWADDYWADDY

The group's name, which is a close kin to Sha Na Na, is taken from the sound of a popular doo-wop backing vocal.

SILVERCHAIR

The most accepted theory about the band's name is that they were all listening to the radio when they decided to call in and request some songs. One of them wrote down the songs they wanted to request; "Sliver" by Nirvana and "Berlin Chair" by the Australian group You Am I. "Sliver" was misspelled as silver and the other song was shortened from "Berlin Chair" to just chair. It came out as silverchair.

SIMPLE MINDS

The group took their name from a line in the David Bowie song "Jean Genie."

SIMPLY RED

"Red" was a childhood nickname given to vocalist Mick Hucknall because of his red hair. Hucknall sang one night at a club where he was a DJ and the manager of the club misheard him and introduced him as "Simply Red" instead of just "Red."

SIOUXSIE AND THE BANSHEES

This name is a combination of lead singer Siouxsie Sioux, born Susan Dallion, and part of the title from a Vincent Price movie *Cry of the Banshee*. A banshee is an Irish ghost of death.

SIGUE SIGUE SPUTNIK

The name comes from a Moscow street gang spotted by a reporter for the *International Herald Tribune*.

SIR DOUGLAS QUINTET

The name was selected to pass the group off as a British invasion band.

THE SISTERS OF MERCY

The Sisters of Mercy is an order of nuns, but the name was taken from a Leonard Cohen song about prostitutes.

SKID ROW

Rachel and Snake were driving home from band practice and throwing potential names into the air. They saw some skid marks on the road and one jokingly suggested, "How about Skid Marks?" The other remarked, "More like skid row," a reference to their financial situation at the time.

SKINNY PUPPY

The name was selected to underscore the group's vision of the world as seen through the eyes of a starving mongrel dog.

SMALL FACES

"Faces" was a slang term for cool or popular people in the 1960's mod scene. Marriot, Lane and Company felt they were physically small examples of this term.

SMASHING PUMPKINS

The name came about as a joke. The band hates being asked what their name means and refuses to tell the story.

SMITHEREENS

The name was taken from the oft-quoted cartoon icon, Yosemite Sam: "I'll blow you varmints to smithereens."

THE SMITHS

Lead singer Morrissey came up with the name. They settled on the simplistic name in response to the popularity of long band names at that time.

SNOOP DOGGY DOGG

Calvin Broadus acquired his nickname from his resemblance to the character Snoopy from the *Peanuts* cartoon strip. His father said that Snoop "had a lot of hair on his head as a baby and looked like a little dog."

SOCIAL DISTORTION

From an internet fan of the group comes this story: "Well, there is society, you see, and they are distorting it."

THE SOFT BOYS

This name is the result of merging two titles by author William Burroughs: *The Soft Machine* and *The Wild Boys*.

SOFT MACHINE

The band took their name from a novel of the same name by William Burroughs.

SON VOLT

In an interview, one of the band founder's response when asked how they came up with the band name was, "It was just a couple of words."

SONIC YOUTH

The name was created by mixing the names of two other local musical groups, "Sonic Rendezvous Orchestra" and "Big Youth."

SOUL ASYLUM

A fan with a web site on the group reported that "all I know is it came to Dave [Pirner] in a dream. Beyond that it's anyone's guess."

SOUL COUGHING

Singer M. Doughty wrote a bad poem about Neil Young throwing up. The poem, entitled "Soul Coughing," became the band's name.

SOUNDGARDEN

The name came from a sculpture in Magnusson Park in Seattle, Washington. The sculpture consists of pipes, hollows and windmill type blades. When the wind blows, the forms of the sculpture cause a low humming sound. The sculpture is titled A Sound Garden.

SPANDAU BALLET

Spandau is an area in Berlin which was the home to a ballet in the 1800s. A friend of the band saw the name on a bathroom wall.

SPARKS

One of the owners of their first record label, Bearsville Records, suggested the group call themselves The Sparks Brothers (a takeoff on the Marx Brothers). The group decided to keep the sparks and lose the brothers.

THE SPECIALS

The name was taken from the special one-shot records made to play on early Jamaican sound systems.

SPICE GIRLS

Gerri came up with the name Spice for the group, which had to be modified to the Spice Girls because another rapper was already using the name Spice.

SPINAL TAP

The band was originally a fictional group created from the Rob Reiner rockumentary movie of the same name. Band members were reportedly in search of a name that sounded painful. Ironically, they thought they were misspelling it. They were under the impression that the procedure was spelled *spynal* tap.

SPIRIT

Originally called Spirits Rebellious after a book by Kahlil Gibran, the band later shortened the name to Spirit.

SQUEEZE

The name was chosen from several names placed in a hat by the group's members. For a time they were Squeeze UK because a band in the US was using the same name.

SQUIRREL NUT ZIPPERS

A Squirrel Nut Zipper is an old-time brand of chewy peanut-flavored candy which contains caramel and nuts. The candy has been made in Cambridge, Massachusetts, since the late 1920s.

STABBING WESTWARD

The band came up with the name in 1985 while attending Western Illinois University. Several of the members worked at a college radio station and wrote down the liner notes of all the albums in the station they thought were clever. Since they went to Western Illinois University, they thought that "stabbing westward" had a certain "kill everybody in the school" vibe to it.

STANDELLS

Standell is the name of a guitar amplifier.

STARRY-EYED AND LAUGHING

The name is borrowed from a line in the Bob Dylan song "Chimes of Freedom."

STARS OF HEAVEN

This name is from a biblical quotation: "I will multiply thy seed as the stars of heaven. And as the sand which is upon the seashore." Genesis 22:17

STATUS QUO

Chosen by the group's manager, Pat Barlow, it was a phrase he kept reading about in the papers and hearing on the "telly." He thought it would stick in people's minds.

STEELY DAN

The name is taken from a steam-powered vibrator in William Burroughs's novel *Naked Lunch*.

STEPPENWOLF

Steppenwolf is the title of a novel by German writer Hermann Hesse.

STIFF LITTLE FINGERS

The name is taken from a Vibrators song referring to a 1960's science fiction series, *The Invaders*. The series was about evil aliens that were identical to humans with the notable exception of their unbendable pinky fingers.

STING

As a teenager, Gordon Matthew Sumner was dubbed "Sting" by the older musicians he was playing with in a traditional jazz band, and it stuck. "It's a stupid name, but I'm used to it," he reported. Another version of the story tells that Sting gained his unusual nickname early in his career: "I wore outrageous, striped, yellow and black pullovers," he told an interviewer, "and one guy thought I looked like a bee. The name stuck."

THE STONE ROSES

A combination of the Rolling Stones, the members' favorite group, and their original name, English Rose.

STONE TEMPLE PILOTS

The name was selected "because it sounded good," says drummer Eric Kretz. The name reportedly came about because of singer Scott Weiland's unusual attachment to an oval STP oil sticker he kept on his bike.

THE STRAWBERRY ALARM CLOCK

The band's label required them to pick a name with "strawberry" in it. While they were brainstorming to find a name, an alarm clock in the room went off and fell to the floor. They all thought this was hilarious and decided to join strawberry with "alarm clock."

STRAWBS

This name is short for the Strawberry Hill Boys. Strawberry Hill is a district in London where the band rehearsed.

THE STRAY CATS

The group regularly changed their names to avoid club owners' attempts to blackball certain groups they didn't like. They kept the word "cats" in each of the various incarnations to clue in their fans that it was the same group.

STYX

The band named themselves after the river in the Greek mythological underworld of Hades.

SUPERTRAMP

The name was taken from the book, *Autobiography of a Supertramp*, written in 1908 by W.H. Davies. The book is a tale of a British tramp who roamed the United States.

SUPREMES

Originally the Primettes, at the urging of Berry Gordy, Florence Ballard selected Supremes from a list supplied by a Motown employee.

SWEET

The band chose the name Sweet because it reflected exactly what they were not.

SWING OUT SISTER

The band named themselves after a b-movie of the 1940s.

T. REX

T. Rex is an abbreviated version of the name of one of the largest dinosaurs, the Tyrannosaurus Rex.

T'PAU

T'Pau is the name of a Vulcan matriarch in the 1967 *Star Trek* episode, "Amok Time," written by Theodore Sturgeon.

TALKING HEADS

This band's name is actually a euphemism for television journalists.

THE TEARDROP EXPLODES

The name came from a caption in the Marvel comic *Daredevil*: "Filling in the park with an unearthly whine—painting the leaf-bare branches with golden fire—the teardrop explodes...."

TEARS FOR FEARS

The name was lifted from a line in the Arthur Janov novel *The Primal Scream*.

TELEVISION

The band chose the name at random during a brainstorm-ing session.

THE TEMPTATIONS

Blurted out by founding member Otis Williams during a break in a recording session, the group's original name, the Elgins, was already taken, forcing them to decide on a new name.

TEN YEARS AFTER

Formed in England in 1966, their name is a reference to the birth of rock music a decade earlier.

TESLA

The name was taken from the little-known inventor of the radio, Nikola Tesla. Although the invention of the radio had long been attributed to Guglielmo Marconi, in 1943, the Supreme Court decided that Nikola Tesla had, in fact, invented modern radio technology. The court ruled that Marconi actually received his patents in "anticipation" of an invention that he had yet to make work and therefore it was Tesla who actually invented radio. Ironically, five months before this decision, Nikola Tesla died alone and destitute in a New York hotel room.

TEXAS

Formed in Glasgow, Scotland, the band took their name from Wim Wenders's 1984 film, *Paris, Texas*.

THAT PETROL EMOTION

Founding member Sean O'Neill told *Rolling Stone*, "Our name is deliberately meant to sum up a whole feeling of frustration and anger that you feel living there [in Northern Ireland]."

THE THE

Rolling Stone claims that the name has created problems for founder Matt Johnson, but he "likes the ambiguous handle. It doesn't suggest any particular preconceptions."

THEY MIGHT BE GIANTS

The name was taken from a little-known 1972 film starring George C. Scott and Joanne Woodward.

THIN LIZZY

The name is an alteration of the character Tin Lizzie from an English comic book. Tin Lizzie was a small female robot, and originally was the nickname of Henry Ford's mass-produced Model T automobile.

THIS MORTAL COIL

The name comes from a line in Shakespeare's *Hamlet:* "For in that sleep of death what dreams may come, when we have shuffled off this mortal coil, must give us pause."

THE THOMPSON TWINS

The Thompson Twins were originally comic strip detectives in the cartoon *Tin Tin.*

THREE DOG NIGHT

The name comes from an Australian expression for a very cold night. Sleeping next to a dog will keep you warm on a cold night. The colder the night, the more dogs you need.

THROBBING GRISTLE

The Yorkshire band took their name from local slang for an erection.

TIN MACHINE

This name came from a song of the same name that the group had written.

TOAD THE WET SPROCKET

The group's name was taken from the name of a make-believe band in a Monty Python skit. The comedy skit appears on Monty Python's *Contractual Obligation Album.*

TOM JONES

Born Thomas Woodward, he was renamed by manager Gordon Mills after the swashbuckling hero of the Henry Fielding novel which had recently been a hit film.

TOM PETTY AND THE HEARTBREAKERS

The story is printed in a pamphlet included in the "Play-back" box set. "After playing in Gainesville, Florida, the group, then called 'Mudcrutch', decided to travel and reside in LA (c. 1974) because that was where they were to make it big. After Mudcrutch fell apart due to conflicts of interest, the group's producer was insightful enough to let Tom take the reigns. Anyone from Mudcrutch was allowed to stay under the condition that Tom lead the band. Denny Cordell was asked to introduce Tom Petty to some acquaintances at a recording studio one day and then referred to the other players as 'The Heartbreakers.' The name stuck."

TOM TOM CLUB

The band was named after the hall where the group rehearsed.

TOMMY JAMES AND THE SHONDELLS

Born Thomas Gregory Jackson, Tommy James formed the Shondells in 1960. Shondell was chosen by James because it was two syllables that sounded musical together.

TOO MUCH JOY

These were reportedly the only words written on a pad of paper the morning after the group's hallucinogenic mushroom-enhanced brainstorming session.

TOOL

In a 1994 interview, Danny says that the band's name stands for how they want their music to be—a tool to aid in understanding lachrymology.

TOTO

Toto is the name of the pet dog of Dorothy from the classic movie, *Wizard of Oz*.

TRAFFIC

The name was chosen by Jim Capaldi as he stood on a corner watching cars pass by.

TRIFFIDS

Triffids are nasty plant monsters who attack the Earth in *The Day of the Triffids*, a 1951 film by John Wyndham.

THE TROGGS

The band's name is short for troglodytes.

THE TUBES

The name was chosen from the terms in a medical dictionary for the bones of the inner ear—tubes, rods and bulbs.

Rock and Roll Call

THE TURTLES
Originally the Crosswind Singers, the name was suggested by their manager as a takeoff on the Byrds.

U2
Bassist Adam Clayton liked XTC's name and a friend suggested U2 as a "slightly ambiguous" name. Lead singer Bono took his stage name (originally Bonovox) from a local store which sold hearing aids. Lead guitarist The Edge reportedly received his name from Bono as a reference to the shape of his head.

UB40
Their name is a reference to the number on the British unemployment benefits card. The name also served as an indication of the band's financial situation at the time.

UGLY KID JOE
The name was inspired by Pretty Boy Floyd, another local band for which they were opening.

ULTRAVOX
Ultravox is Latin and means "many voices."

UNIT 4+2
In the 1960s in Britain, the music chart rundown was divided into units 1-4. The group was originally called Unit

4 referring to this chart organization. Two more people joined to make them +2.

URGE OVERKILL
This name was taken from a quote on a Parliament record.

VAN DER GRAAF GENERATOR
This purposefully misspelled name was chosen in 1967 by the band's founder Chris Judge Smith. The name memorializes R.J. Van de Graaff's invention of a static electricity generator used in atomic energy research.

VANILLA FUDGE
The name reflected that the band was a bunch of white guys primarily performing R & B music. A girl in a club suggested the name after hearing them play.

VELVET UNDERGROUND
The group chose their name from the pulp novel of the same name about the joys of sado-masochism.

THE VENTURES
Originally the Versatones, they changed their name to reflect their "new adventure."

VERUCA SALT
Veruca Salt was a character in the novel *Charlie and the Chocolate Factory*, later made into a film starring Gene

Wilder called *Willie Wonka and the Chocolate Factory*.

THE VIOLENT FEMMES

The name was suggested by one of the members when the photographer for their first record album questioned them about what their brother did. The member was lying to the photographer and got caught without a quick response when asked by the photographer what group his brother played in. He blurted out, "The Violent Femmes."

W.A.S.P.

The name is an acronym for We Are Sexual Perverts.

WALL OF VOODOO

Wall of Voodoo is a takeoff on Phil Spector's "Wall of Sound."

THE WALLFLOWERS

Rumor has it that the band took their name from a song written years ago by Jakob Dylan's father, Bob Dylan. The song is called "Wallflower."

WANG CHUNG

Formerly Huang Chung, which is Chinese for "Perfection in Music," the name was later changed to Wang Chung.

WAR

In the middle of the peace movement in the late 1960s, the name was chosen to attract people's attention.

WAS (NOT WAS)

Founding members Don Was (born Don Fagenson) and David Was (born David Weiss) chose the name during a period in which Don Was's child was beginning to understand the concept of opposites.

WAYNE FONTANA AND THE MINDBENDERS

Originally the band was called the Mindbenders after *The Mind Benders*, a film starring Dirk Bogarde. Lead singer Wayne Fontana, born Glyn Geoffrey Ellis, renamed himself in honor of Fontana Records, the band's first label.

WEEN

The name is a cross between "wuss" and "peen" from "penis."

WEEZER

Supposedly, the name was lifted from the character "Weezer" in the television show "The Little Rascals."

WET, WET, WET

This name comes from the line "his face is wet, wet with tears" taken from the Scritti Politti song "Getting, Having, and Holding." The third wet was added to distinguish them from other names of the time (e.g. Duran Duran, Talk Talk, etc.).

WHAM!

The name was taken from the band's early composition, "Wham Rap," which has the line "Wham, Bam, I am a man!"

WHITE ZOMBIE

The group was named after a 1932 Bela Lugosi movie.

WHITESNAKE

The name was taken from the title of a failed album by singer David Coverdale, which he cut soon after his exit from Deep Purple in 1976.

THE WHO

The name was chosen because it would print up big on concert posters and cause enough confusion to be memorable. Pete Townshend originally suggested the name The Hair and the Who.

WINGS

The name was chosen by founder Paul McCartney and inspired by the difficult birth his second child, Stella. McCartney prayed that his child would be delivered on the wings of angels.

THE WONDER STUFF
Band member Miles Hunt's father often hosted John Lennon when Miles was a child. He told Miles that Lennon used to refer to Miles's running around the house, saying, "That kid sure has the wonder stuff."

WOODENTOPS
The group was named after a children's television puppet show.

THE WU-TANG CLAN
One of the deadliest of all kung fu styles was the famed Wu-Tang sword, an invincible weapon mastered only by accomplished monks. The name is taken from this style.

X
Named in honor of the band's singer Exene Cervenka.

XTC
The name is a phonetic rendering of "ecstasy."

THE YARDBIRDS
The band was named in honor of the famous saxophonist, Charlie "Yardbird" Parker.

YELLO
"Yello" is a yelled "Hello."

YES

In the liner notes to a Yes box set, singer Jon Anderson recounts the story: "Yes got pulled out of the bag, I think. We wanted to display a strong conviction in what we were doing. We had to have a strong and straight title for the band."

YO LA TENGO

The name means "I have it" or "I have her" in Spanish.

THE YOUNGBLOODS

The band was named after founder Jesse Colin Young.

ZZ TOP

According to drummer Frank Beard, ironically the only member of the band who doesn't have a beard, the name is a parody of B.B. King. "We just wanted a name that sounded like maybe some crusty old blues player."

Another story suggests that the name is taken from the names of two brands of rolling papers.

A third story suggests that the name was chosen to put them in the last bin at record shops—easy to find.

ABOUT THE AUTHOR

Dean Boland is a father and husband who, along with his wife, Lisa, and daughter, Abby, is enjoying life in Lakewood, Ohio, a suburb of Cleveland. He works as an Assistant Prosecuting Attorney for the Cuyahoga County Prosecutor's office in Cleveland and authors a monthly column on law and technology for the *Cleveland Bar Journal.*

Dean is a third degree black belt in Soo Bahk Do Moo Duk Kwan, a Korean martial art, and has trained for over twelve years. His undergraduate degree from Cleveland State University is in Anthhropology.

Other titles available from

Dowling Press

The Walrus Was Paul:

The Great Beatle Death Clues of 1969

by R. Gary Patterson

0-9646452-1-1 $16.95/Paper/6 x 9/160 pp.

In the fall of 1969, the sinister news that Paul McCartney had been decapitated in an automobile accident flooded American radio airways. The idea that some hidden conspiracy existed to hide the truth from an unsuspecting public brought back repressed memories of the JFK assassination and the everyday uncertainty of the Cold War. Some of the death clues were hilarious, while some, in an attempt to find anything to substantiate the ghoulish rumor, were ridiculous. However, several of the clues were obviously planted by the Beatles themselves and remain unanswered to this day.

"The Walrus Was Paul is loaded....mind-blowing stuff from the best Beatle book yet!"

—Jim Zippo, ABC Radio Network.

Ticket to Ride:

The Extraordinary Diary of The Beatles' Last Tour

by Barry Tashian

0-9646452-4-6 $19.95/Paper/11 x 8 ½/ 160 pp.

Thirty years after The Beatles performed together live for the last time, Barry Tashian, lead singer of The Remains, the opening band on The Beatles' last tour, has compiled **Ticket to Ride: The Extraordinary Diary of The Beatles' Last Tour**. **Ticket to Ride** contains Tashian's tour journal and never-before-seen photographs of The Beatles, both onstage and behind the scenes.

"Ticket to Ride is the chronicle of the ending of one era of popular music and the heralding of the 'next phase.' I *highly recommend* **Ticket to Ride: The Extraordinary Diary of The Beatles' Last Tour** to all Beatles fans and pop music lovers. Grab your ticket and enjoy the ride."

—Francis Bell, **The Music Paper**

Cheese Chronicles:

The Story of A Rock 'n' Roll Band

You've Never Heard Of

by Tommy Womack

0-9646452-3-8 $14.95/Paper/6 x 9/304 pp.

Heralded as a must-read for anybody playing rock and roll in their basement or garage, hoping to make it big in music, Womack takes readers on tour with his band, Government Cheese.

"*Cheese Chronicles* is the best street-level book on being in a rock and roll band, ever."

–The Reverend Keith A. Gordon

"Womack is a gifted writer, a child of the Seventies, and he sounds like a Holden of *Catcher in the Rye*. The pathos is missing, but he fills the space with hilarious comedy, and a sense of the absurdity of life that makes playing in a rock band the most logical choice of career possible."

—Kay Kimbrough, *The Harbinger*, Mobile, Alabama

A Lifetime of Rules on Dating Women

by Gavin Reily and Louis Vale

0-9646452-2-X $5.95/Paper/5 x 5/128 pp.

A Lifetime of Rules on Dating Women contains over four hundred sure-fire, tried-and-true tips to follow when dating. The book explores the first date through the hundredth date, explains how to kiss and how to break up, and covers just about everything in between. Humorous, yet sensitive, serious, but lighthearted, *A Lifetime of Rules on Dating Women* is brimming over with great advice, a must for anyone who has taken part in that wonderful but sometimes unpredictable human ritual: dating.

Thanks for the Mammaries:
The Naked Truth About Pregnancy

by Tina Hooper

0-9646452-7-0 $6.95/Paper/5 x 5/124 pp./25 illustrations
Thanks for the Mammaries is a side-splitting collection of the
"untold truths" about being pregnant. Written by Tina
Hooper, this book contains 101 funny facts that will surely
entertain anyone who has been, is, or wants to be pregnant.
Peppered with hilarious cartoons, ***Thanks for the***
Mammaries is the complete guide for expectant mothers
who want to laugh between trips to the bathroom.

Jealous Heart

by Cecelia Tishy

0-9646452-5-4 $24.00/Hardcover/ 348 pp./6 x 9
When Boston native Kate Banning is offered a job with
Fleetwood Publications in Nashville, she chooses to move
with some trepidation. Kate, a former investigative journalist
from Boston, is all too familiar with occupational hazards,
and determined to start a new life—a new beginning for her
teenage daughter Kelly and herself. Soon, however, Kate
finds that Nashville is not the peaceful slow-moving Southern town she expects, but has a very dark side teeming with
deceit, rage, and desire. Brandi Burns, a rising country
music starlet, is killed in a car accident, her young life and
promising career tragically cut short. Soon, Kate realizes
that the fatal accident was really no accident at all, and it is
up to her to launch a pulse-racing chase to find the killer
with the *Jealous Heart*.

"Cecelia Tishy's ***Jealous Heart*** is a fast-paced country
rocker debut that captures the mean streets of Music Row—
where people will literally kill for a song—beautifully. Kate
Banning's a wonderful character and a delightful new voice
in Southern mystery!"

—Steven Womack, Edgar Award-winning author of *Chain of*
Fools.

coming this fall from

HELLHOUNDS ON THEIR TRAIL
TALES FROM THE ROCK N ROLL GRAVEYARD

by R. Gary Patterson.

ISBN: 0-9646452-6-2

Specifications: 5.5 by 8.25, 224 pp. pb

$15.95

It seems that mankind has always been fascinated with the dark side — the primeval forces that provided the bogeyman in our closets and the loathsome creatures under our beds. These forces have helped formulate some of the most traumatic fears of our young lives. It seems that the age-old concept of good versus evil, God versus Satan, has become the archaic theme that teaches the moralist to live. Shakespeare's main characters struggle with the obligation to fight for order and resist the temptation to succumb to temporal earthly gratifications: money, power, and sex.

In Marriage of Heaven and Hell, William Blake writes "the road to excess leads to the palace of wisdom." Hellhounds on Their Trail is a study of rock music's most prominent icons who have crossed the fine line between reality and mythology and whose stories depict the struggle between new-found success and waiting tragedy. Through each of their successes, each has symbolically waited at legendary bluesman Robert Johnson's crossroads to choose his or her destiny. In turn, each became a victim in "the fell clutch of circumstance." These stories will become a staple of urban legend.

To order, call 1-800-243-9230